DEMAND AND SUPPLY VIEW IN SOCIAL ECONOMY

JOHN LOK

Contents

Foreword

Introduction

In our societies , any kinds of products or services must need to apply demand and supply economic theory to analyze whether the kind of product or service may be value to invent to sell or serve to their customers in consumer market, if the kind of product or service demand number is less, then it ought not to raise manufacturing number to avoid "low price " sale or if the kind of product demand number is more, then it ought raise manufacturing number to have enough number in order to raise " high price" sale to satisfy customers their needs to buy their products.
However, whether your product or serive's demand number depends on supply number or your product or service's supply number depends on demand number in order to make ths sale price is reasonable high or low level and reasonable supply number valuation.
In my this book, I shall indicate some actual product or service social suitation to explain whether these kinds of product or service is depended on either demand or supply aspect more in behavioral economic view.

Prologue

Contents

Chapter 5 Technology demand and supply relationship
Can technology influence human shopping behavioral change?
p.91-130
Why and how human behavior may influence the country's economic growth or recession?
Technology how impacts human behavior changing?
How and why employees behaviors may influence economy development?
Robots invention whether they can help organizations to raise efficiencies or inefficiencies?
Why social behavior may influence organizational strategy needs to be changed ?
How and why human behavior may influence economic growth or recession?

Chapter 6 Illness how influence leisure online shopping demand and supply changes

How COVID 19 disease influences tourism leisure need

Why COV19 disease and traveller traveelling lesiure behavior have close relationship ?
p.131-145

Why COVID 19 disease influences travellers begin to concern green or nature tourism ?

How COVID 19 disease influences tourism industry recession ?

Why senior age will be main travelling target after COV19 disease attacks to global tourism lesiure need?

What are the characteristics of future tourism industry changes after COVID 19 disease disappears?

How to develop new economic tourism industry after COVID 19 disease disappears ?

How COVID 19 disease influences space tourism industry development

Why does the space tourism leisure need may raise after COVID 19 disease disappears ?
p.146-156

Why does COVD19 disease influences future space tourism leisure need raises?

How COVID disease influences global oil need and price change to impact travelling lesisure industry development

How does price factor won't be the main factor to influence space traveler number when COVID 19 disease brings negative emotion to travellers ? p.157-170

Can COVID 19 disease influence Space travel marketing strategy changes?

Airport service life cycle stage improvement strategy can improve future tourism industry to grow up after COVID 19 disease disappears ?

How COVID 19 disease influences cruise leisure need

How COVID 19 disease influences cruise pasengers their tourism leisure on sea to Singapre and Australia cruise leisure passengers number and medical insurace expense is raised ? p.171-180

Can COVI19 disease cause the cruise industry service staffs lose jobs?

How cruise travelers can protect themselves ?

Illness how influences Online Shopping Behavior Develops

COVID 19 disease how influences consumer individual visiting shopping behavior p.181-200

COVID 19 disease how brings online shopping behavior chance

COVID 19 disease how impacts global economic recession on shopping aspect

When economy recovers after COVID disease disappears

CHAPTER ONE

EXPLAINING SUPPLY AND DEMAND ECONOMIC THEORY RELATIONSHIP

The difference between past and nowadays economists their demand and supply economic theory explanation?

The law of supply and demand defines the relationship between the price of a given good or product and the willingness of people to either buy or sell it. Generally, as the price of a good increases, people are willing to supply more and demand less. These economists had explained economic demand and supply theory as below:

Philosopher John Locke is credited with one of the earliest written descriptions of this economic principle in his 1691 publication, Some Considerations of the Consequences of the Lowering of Interest and the Raising of the Value of Money. Locke addressed the concept of supply and demand as part of a discussion about interest rates in 17th-century England. Many merchants wanted the government to lower the cap on interest rates charged by private lenders so that people could borrow more money and thus purchase more goods. Locke argued that the free-market economy should set rates because government regulation could have unintended consequences. If the lending industry were left alone, interest rates would regulate themselves, Locke wrote: "The price of any commodity rises or falls by the proportion of the number of buyers and sellers."

Sir James Steuart's Inquiry into the Principles of Political Economy, published in 1796, was the first known printed use of the term "supply and demand." When Steuart wrote his treatise on political economy, one of his main concerns was the impact of supply and demand on laborers.

Adam Smith dealt extensively with the topic in his 1776 epic economic work, The Wealth of Nations. Often referred to as the Father of Economics, Smith explained the concept of supply and demand as an "invisible hand" that naturally guides the economy. According to Smith, the invisible hand is the automatic pricing and distribution mechanisms in the economy. Smith described a society in which bakers and butchers provide products that individuals need and want, providing a supply that meets demand and developing an economy that benefits everyone. It is important to note that Smith's ideas haven't gone without critique over the years since his ideas were first published, though. Over time, his ideas have been added to in order to represent the changing times and include concepts such as marginal utility, comparative advantage, entrepreneurship, the time-preference theory of interest, and monetary theory.

One of Marshall's most important contributions to microeconomics was his introduction of the concept of price elasticity of demand, which examines how price changes affect demand. In theory, people buy less of a particular product if the price increases, but Marshall noted that in real life, this behavior was not always true. The prices of some goods can increase without reducing demand, which means their prices are inelastic. Inelastic goods tend to include items such as medication or food that consumers deem crucial to daily life. Marshall argued that supply and demand, costs of production, and price elasticity all work together.

Nowadays economists they explain demand and supply economic theory, they have some different to past economists whose explanation as below:

How Does Supply and Demand Work? The law of supply and demand is a theory that explains the interaction between the sellers of a resource and the buyers of that resource. Generally, as price increases, people are willing to supply more and demand less and vice versa when the price falls.

What does the bottom line mean. Despite the origins of the law of supply and demand beginning hundreds of years ago, it's still a topic frequently referenced and utilized today in economic theory and discussions. The theory has developed over time to accommodate recent technological and economical advancements, but the basic ideas of the theory remain largely the same.

Does demand depend on supply?
Supply and Demand Determine the Price of Goods and Quantities Produced and Consumed. Consumers may exhaust the available supply of a good by purchasing a given good or service at a high volume. This leads to an increase in demand. As demand increases, the available supply also decreases.
What does market demand depend on?
Market factors affecting demand of consumer goods. The demand for a good increases or decreases depending on several factors. This includes the product's price, perceived quality, advertising spend, consumer income, consumer confidence, and changes in taste and fashion.
Who controls the demand in supply and demand?
Supply and demand are in turn determined by technology and the conditions under which people operate. At one extreme, the market could be populated by a large number of virtually identical sellers and buyers (for example, the market for ballpoint pens).
What are the two laws of demand and supply?
The law of demand holds that the demand level for a product or a resource will decline as its price rises, and rise as the price drops. Conversely, the law of supply says higher prices boost supply of an economic good while lower ones tend to diminish it.
What factors affect demand and supply?
Price fluctuations are a strong factor affecting supply and demand. When a product gets expensive enough that the average consumer no longer feels it is worth it to buy the product, then the demand declines. This leads to cuts in production that will hopefully stabilize the product's value.
What factors affect demand and demand?
Demand may be defined as the quantity of a commodity that a consumer is able and willing to buy, at each possible price, over a given period of time. • Essential elements of demand are quantity, ability, willingness, prices, and period of time.
Which factors affect supply?
Generally, the supply of a product depends on its price and other variables such as the cost of production.

a. Price. Price can be understood as what the consumer is willing to pay to receive a good or service. ...
b. Cost of production. ...
c. Technology. ...

d. Governments' policies. ...
e. Transportation condition.
How does supply and demand work together?
It's a fundamental economic principle that when supply exceeds demand for a good or service, prices fall. When demand exceeds supply, prices tend to rise. There is an inverse relationship between the supply and prices of goods and services when demand is unchanged.
What happens to supply when demand increases?
An increase in demand, all other things unchanged, will cause the equilibrium price to rise; quantity supplied will increase. A decrease in demand will cause the equilibrium price to fall; quantity supplied will decrease.
What is the theory of demand?
Demand theory describes the way that changes in the quantity of a good or service demanded by consumers affects its price in the market, The theory states that the higher the price of a product is, all else equal, the less of it will be demanded, inferring a downward sloping demand curve.
What are the 4 basic laws of supply and demand?
1) If the supply increases and demand stays the same, the price will go down. 2) If the supply decreases and demand stays the same, the price will go up. 3) If the supply stays the same and demand increases, the price will go up. 4) If the supply stays the same and demand decreases, the price will go down.
The different types of demand are as follows:
i. Individual and Market Demand: ...
ii. Organization and Industry Demand: ...
iii. Autonomous and Derived Demand: ...
iv. Demand for Perishable and Durable Goods: ...
v. Short-term and Long-term Demand:
What creates demand for a product?
You can create demand for a unique product if you can manage to solve a persistent problem for the consumer. People are always running away from pain, and providing them with an outlet is a sure-fire way to create massive demand for your goods.
What are the 7 factors that affect supply?
The seven factors which affect the changes of supply are as follows: (i) Natural Conditions (ii) Technical Progress (iii) Change in Factor Prices (iv) Transport Improvements (v) Calamities (vi) Monopolies (vii) Fiscal Policy.

What can affect demand?
Factors Affecting Demand
Price of the Product. ...
The Consumer's Income. ...
The Price of Related Goods. ...
The Tastes and Preferences of Consumers. ...
The Consumer's Expectations. ...
The Number of Consumers in the Market.
What are the three factors affecting demand?
The demand for a product will be influenced by several factors:
Price. Usually viewed as the most important factor that affects demand. ...
Income levels. ...
Consumer tastes and preferences. ...
Competition. ...
Fashions.
What are the 4 factors of supply?
The four factors that can shift the supply curve include natural conditions, input prices, technology, and government.
What causes increase in supply?
If the cost of production is lower, the profits available at a given price will increase, and producers will produce more. With more produced at every price, the supply curve will shift to the right, meaning an increase in supply.
What causes supply changes?
A change in supply is an economic term that describes when the suppliers of a given good or service alter production or output. A change in supply can occur as a result of new technologies, such as more efficient or less expensive production processes, or a change in the number of competitors in the market.
Is supply and demand a good strategy?
When it comes to profit placement, supply and demand zones can be a great tool as well. Always place your profit target ahead of a zone so that you don't risk giving back all your profits when the open interest in that zone is filled.
How is demand created?
Demand creation is a process that fuels the revenue pipeline so the sales team can meet or exceed their quotas. In other words, it takes your big idea — the creative appeal of your brand — and turns it into sales. That sounds a

lot like demand generation, which often gets confused with lead generation.
What are the two parts of demand?
Economists define demand as the quantity of a good or service that buyers are willing and able to buy at all possible prices during a certain time period. Notice that there are two components to demand: willingness to purchase and ability to pay.
Can we control demand?
If you're willing to think and act strategically, you can easily manipulate the laws of supply and demand. It should be surprising to learn, however, that by manipulating the laws of supply and demand, you can make more profit in less time and with far fewer headaches
How do you control demand?
Here are five short-term actions to improve your demand variability management plans in this time of uncertainty:

Maintain transparent, proactive relationships with your suppliers. ...
Activate alternate sources of supply. ...
Reduce lead times. ...
Update inventory policy and planning. ...
Align supply and demand management.
What are the 8 types of demand?
There are 8 states of demand: negative demand, no demand, latent demand, falling demand, irregular demand, full demand, overfull demand and unwholesome demand.
What is Demand?

Types of Determinants of Demand. Every factor has a unique impact on demand. ...
Price of the Product. ...
The Income of the Consumers. ...
Number of Buyers in the Market. ...
Consumer's Expectations. ...
Tastes and Preferences of The Consumers. ...
Complement Goods. ...
Substitute Product.
What is theory of supply?
The law of supply is a fundamental principle of economic theory which states that, keeping other factors constant, an increase in price results in an increase in quantity supplied. In other words, there is a direct relationship between price and quantity: quantities respond in the same direction as

price changes.

What are the types of supply?

There are five types of supply—market supply, short-term supply, long-term supply, joint supply, and composite supply.

Which comes first supply or demand?

Demand comes first and it's followed by the corresponding supplies. Supply and demand are both very important to economic activity. Supply is the total amount of a particular good or service available at a given time to consumers at a given price. Demand is a representation of a consumer's desire to purchase goods and services; it acts as a measurement of a consumer's willingness to purchase a specific good or service at a given price. These two economic forces influence each other; they are both important for the economy because they impact the prices of consumer goods and services within an economy and the quantities produced and consumed. Supply and demand are both keys to understanding the economy because they reflect the prices and quantities of consumer goods and services within an economy.

What are the relationship between demand and supply?

According to market economy theory, the relationship between supply and demand balances out at a point in the future; this point is called the equilibrium price.

Economists and companies analyze the relationship between supply and demand when making strategic product decisions. Both economists and companies analyze the relationship between supply and demand when making strategic product decisions. The assumption behind a market economy is that supply and demand are the best determinants for an economy's growth and health.

Consumer Behavior Influences Demand

One way that companies or economists might analyze this relationship is to create graphs that chart the equilibrium price of certain goods and services in order to determine product development and their production schedule. Consumer behavior dictates which products are produced and sold because consumers create the demand that companies attempt to meet. As a result, companies may study consumer behavior in an attempt to understand the current demand and predict future demand. It is vital that companies maintain the capacity to produce enough of a good or service that they can satisfy consumer demands.

Supply and demand are two sides of the same market coin. Generally, supply is how much of something is available or will be produced at a certain price. Demand is how much of something people want to purchase or consume at a certain price. One way to develop a more precise relationship between the two is to consider how the price of something affects its supply and its demand. Generally when the price of a good goes up, so does the supply, since firms are willing to create more when they can sell at higher prices. But when the price of a good goes up consumers will, at the same time, generally demand less. It is the interaction of supply and demand that determines how much will be produced and consumed and at what price, converging to a state known as equilibrium.

CHAPTER TWO

EXPLAINING SUPPLY AND DEMAND ECONOMIC THEORY RELATIONSHIP

The relationship between social change and human behavior

Human Behavioral network job brings social economic benefits

Whether human social job change it depends on social job demand more or job supply more? What does human network job mean ? Why may human network job be popular? Why human network job behavior may influence economy ?

Nowadays internet is popular to use. We can apply internet to find data , search any new things, even earn money. Why does internet
may become huma network job source. For example, e-publish may be one kind of new human network job. Any authors may apply internet
channel to help them to sell electronic or paper books from e-publisher web store. They may apply facebook, you tub etc. any online
channel to promote themselves new books to let new readers to know whether when they may buy themselves favourable new topic books to read from electronic publisher web store.

Thus, future electronic publisher industry may help any authors to build internet network platform to help them to sell and promote
ot advertise their any one new electronic or paper book topic to let global

any one reader to choose to buy their any new topic books from electronic publisher web store easily and conveniently. However, it implies that electronic network platform author may be one kind of future new human network job in our societies.

How electronic network platform author job may bring economy benefit in macro economy view? A person can have few friends, contacts and still be very influential if these few
friends and contacts are themselves highly influential, e.g. one author must not need to know any one reader in global society. When they like to choose any electronic books from electronic internet network platform. They may become the author's any one topic book buyer, when they feel the author's any one topic book is fun and attract they make decision to buth the strange author whose the topic book from electronic book publisher's platform web store conventiently in short time. Although, they are strangers, they do not know themselves , but the reader can understand what it way that made Google from writing platofrm to create new creative mind and typing network job method to replace traditional hand writing book method for global authors. It will be one kind of new human network writing job.

Hence, global any one reader can apply an innovative search engine , such as google.com to find whether whom author personal new topic books are value to read from internet.
Then, the electroniuc publisher's web store may be new book store platform sale network to help the author to sell many electronic or paper books from electronic network platform
in short time. So, internet may be future new network plaform to help global any one author to create network writing job absolutely. Furthermore, internet may be popular social media
to help any one author to build goold relationship between his/her readers. It is one kind of new network, human network job. New authors do not need to buy many paper books to prepare to put in any one book shop warehouse. Their every book can print on demand to reduce out of book stock in any one book shop. They may choose to sell either electronic books or paper books both from any one book publisher web store. So, electronic network platform may be one kind of good writing channel to help human authors to create income and it can also help authors to bring new creative mind and new topic fun content books to let readers to know and buy to read from electronic publisher network platform.

Why does human behavior may be one kind of new human network job to bring global economic advantages. ALthough, it may be free income or without inocme, but the person does the network behavior, his/her behavior may be bring advantages to influence many other people's health. For this case, when a worker in a coffee shop in an airport gets a vaccination aganinst the flu, it does not only helps him or her stay healthy, but also helps the many travellers who might otherwise have been inflected if that workers caught the flu. So, the externality , the result implies the vaccination of even a part of a community conveys benefits to the whole community. For example, governments pay special attention to the vaccinations of school children, teachers, health mothers, and the elderly, categories of people particularly susceptible not only to catching, but also to transmitting a disease.

It is not accidential that governments are heavily involved with vaccination . When there are externalities, free market, fail to persuade individual incentives with society's

their the worker's decision of whether to get a vaccine ends up attracting whether other people get sick. The workers might not fully take all these other people's potential suffering into account when making her or his vaccination decision.

As Stanford University does many suggestions, understand this and tries to help them make the right decisions and so providers free flu vaccines for its staff and students.

Small pockets of unvaccinated individuals can allow a disease to gain a spread more widely well-being. For example, parent weighing the costs and benefits of a vaccine for their child is not always thinking of the consequences of that vaccination to other people. THese are markets in which subsidizing or regulating behavior can make everyone better off. Because the reason for requiring that a child be vaccinated before enrolling in school is not just to protect that child, because each child's vaccination affects others via potential contagions.

On conclusion, it seems that many traditional paper book publish business begain to change to electronic book publish business. Due, to online technology existence, it influences many readers choose to buy electronic books to read. Hence, due to readers reading demand change which is from paper book reading habit to electonic book reading habit.Then,it explains that electornic book supply number depends on electronic book reader reading demand in economic view.

Robots take our jobs behavioral and economy influences

Robot job behavior brings economy influences

Whether robot labor needs are depended on employer labor demand more or robot labor number supply more? If one day robots can replace human to do simple, even complex jobs. They will bring what influences to our global societial economy.The popular economic refrain declares that the global middle class is dying and robots will soon take our jobs, e.g. shopping center customer service jobs, library service jobs, cinema ticket sale jobs, restaurant kitchen cooker jobs, even, bus drivers, taxi drivers etc. public transport driving jobs, accountant, doctors etc. professional jobs. Whether it is beautiful or petty matter if our future societies have many human jobs can be replaced to do from robots. Businessman must may reduce to employ employees and reduce to pay salary or wage, when robots can be replaced to do their employees tasks. But, societies must bring unemployement rate rises , due to societies will have many people loss jobs when their employers choose to buy robots to serve their clients or do any office tasks or customer service or cleaning etc. tasks.

In micro economy view, employers may save money in long term, but in macro economy view, it will cause unemployment ratio rises , even crime rate rises when there are many people lose jobs in societies. These models of doom, though, fail to account for the hundreds of businesses riding the waves of change in their industries when robots may be invented to replace human to do many simple , even complex tasks in our future societies.

WE may image that one small factory needs to manufacture fishes canes to sell to supermarket, the small , cheaper stuff and higher margin parts of the fishes manufacture industry. Before, this factory needs to employe many human factory workers need to help every fresh customer makeing the perfect fishing gear, designed for performance, durability, and cost in order to achieve to manufacture every fish cane in whole fished processing manufacturing stages. Every worker needs to spend about 15 to twenty minutes to finish every fish cane , till to delivery to any supermarket to sell. If this fish canes manufacturing factory can apply manufacturing robots to help them to finish any one working tasks , every robot can only spend five

minutes to finish whole fresh fish cane manufacturing process. Thus, every robot can
help this factory save 10 to 15 minutes time to finsh every fish cane manufacturing process. IN fact, time is money, because when every robot can help this factory to reduce 10 to 15 minutes time to compare human worker. Then, this factory can finish about 20 fish canes in one hour if it can use robot to help it to manufacture fish canes. Otherwise, if this factory still use human workers to help it to manufacture fish canes, then it can finsh about 3 to 4 fish canes in one hour. SO, the manufacturing efficiency ensures that robots must help this fish manufacturing factory to raise fish canes number more than human workers. So, in robotic behavioral economy view, manufacturing robots must help this fish canes manufacturing factory to raise fish canes manufacturing number and deliver increasing number to supermarkets to prepare to sell every day. Robots can help this fish canes manufacturing factory bring manufacturing time saving, rising manufacturing efficiency, improving performance and reducing wages expenditure long time advantages in micro economy view. However, manufacturing robots can also bring disadvanages to society, e.g. increasing unemployment ratio, increasing crime rate,
this factory workers will lose jobs and income, they need earn social welfare from government and increasing government finance pressure in short time, even long time in macro economic view.

Stanford University graduate program in economics, Scott lecturer explained that "in demand and supply economic theory for robots supply and demand case, robots supply number increasing may influence human workers demand number decrease. It sometimes calls " the efficient frontier".
No specific human beings were mentioned in any of economics classes. As robots supply and demand in market case, They (robots) may be purely theoretical " agents" who reached to the most reasonable sale prices in order to persuade any one businessman buyer to make manufacturing robot buying decision whether robots can help him / her to bring how much saving time , saving money, saving cost, improving performance, efficiency economic benefit before he/she plans to reduce workers number when he/ she decides to apply robots to replace human workers in his/her factory or office or any service department, e.g. cinema ticket sale service, shopping center customer service, shopping center cleaning , supermarket customer service etc. service or sale tasks. When robots can replace human to do any

one of these tasks in any organizations. So, robots may be human worker agents who reached to prices the way robots would react to a software command. There was nothing that explained why some people thrived and others did n't or why truly brilliant, hardworking people could fail when much lazier folks succeeded." Having been admitted to the Stanford University graduate program in economics, Scott lecturer hoped to get his answers there.

How robots influence our future social changing? Using the right technology can be a boon to your business in this economy. For internet example, it is easier than ever to find well-matched customers all around the world, to stay in contact with them, and to more quickly design the products they want. If you focus solely on being cutting -edge, though you risk letting the technology

take over what should be very robust relationships with your customers , employees, and colleagues. IN nowaddays society, technoligical advances and cutomation, personal

relationships in business are more crucial than ever. I mean that robots can not replace human to serve clients to let them to feel more comfortable and passion more easily. For shoe shop case example, if the shoe shop apply one robot to serve its clients to replace human shoe salesperson to serve its shoe customers. Robots ensure that they can not persuade every shoe potential buyer to make shoe buying decision more easily when robots need to contact every shoe potential buyer. The reason is simple, because robots can not touch any one shoe buyer individual emotion very easier.

If the shoe buyer needs the robots to help him/her to choose any right shoe styles when he/she can not feel himself / herself can make the most right shoe style choice decision. The robots can not replace human shoe salesperson to make shoe style choice judgement more easily. They must need longer time to analyze whether which shoe style may be the most suitable to the shoe buyer. Otherwise, human shoe salesperson may attempt to make the most right shoe style choice decision to help any one shoe buyer to chooce the most right style shoe because he/she owns shoe style sale experience, shoe style knowledge, the most important reason is that they can feel every shoe customer individual emotion to touch whether he/she will feel comfortable or happy when they attempt to help every shoe customer to seek the most right shoe style in every shoe customer whole shoe searching processing. Othwerwise, serving robots are only one machine, they can not touch or feel every shoe customer individual emotion

whether he/she feel comfortable or unhappy or happy when they need to contact them in whole shoe searching processing. Hence, I believe that some tasks robots can
not repalce human staff to do very easily. Otherwise, robots may bring disadvanatges to let any one businessman to loss his/her customers, due to robots can not touch every customer
emotion to compare human staff in service tasks more easily. Robots serving customer behaviors may cause money lose and customers number lose to the shop in micro economic view.

On conclusion, in demand and supply economic theory for robots supply and demand case, robots supply number increasing may influence human workers demand number decrease. So, it seems that robots number supply will be depended on global robots supply number more than robots demand number because when human began to accept robots to replace human to do general simple jobs in global labor market. Then, it means that global robots labor number must need to be increased in order to satisfy global businessmen workers number need. If any kinds of robot workers manufacture number is not enough to be supplied to let global future businessmen to buy, then robot supply will be shortage and they can not provide to satisfy global businessmen robots labour purchase need. So, future robot number will be depended on supply more than demand.

CHAPTER THREE

HUMAN INTELLECTUAL DEMAND AND SUPPLY BEHAVIOR RELATIONSHIP

Intellectual human economic behaviors

What does intellectual human economic behaviors mean ? Human foolish behavior is depended on social enjoyment need more or material social supply more? I believe that when we choose or decide to do intellectual behaviors, then our societies will be influenced to bring economic growth in consequence.I shall attempt to indicate pollution case to explain how and why eithet our intellectual or foolish behaviors may bring economic growth or recession in consequence as below:

On one hand, for air pollution social case aspect example, if we only consider to buy cars to drive for working aim or holiday leisure aim. Then, our societies air will be polluted. Our health will be influenced to bad. Our car driving behaviors may cause global environment air pollution serously. In long tiem, global air pollution will bring our bodies health to be bad. Although, ourselves car driving behaviors may bring our driving travelling leisure enjoyment and comfortable feeling in short time, also we so not need to pay public transport fare often, but we need to compensate ourselves health economic intangible loss due to air pollution , when cars number increases, dirty air will cause ouselves health to become bad.

In the result, we will need to pay more medical expenditure when we are old age, due to ourselves bodies will become bad, due to we breathe global dirty air every day, due to ourselves cars pollute air in long time, e.g. 10 to 20 years, even 30 more without limited air pollution environment. So, driving cars behavior may be one kind of human foolish behavior and our foolish behavior may bring ourselves future long time medical expenditure absolutely.

One the other hand, water pollution social aspect, if we often keep much rubblish to pollute sea, oil exploration porcessing pollute ocean , ships gas pollute ocaen, then fishes will eat polluted food and drive dirty water, due to global ocean is polluted.

In fact, because human only to conside how to buy boats to carry on leisure enjoyment activities, or catch cruises to travel on the sea. Also, oil manufacturers only consider researching anywhere to find new oil exploration places to manufacture oil product, when their oil exploration processes pollute ocarn . Consequently, global fishes drink polluted warer or eat polluted food. They will have poison. SO, human will have high chance to eat poison polluted fishes, due to fishes are poison or are polluted. So, human is doing foolish activities, we only hope to find oil exploration places to pollute ocean or we only spend money to buy ticket to catch ships to travel anywhere in global ocean. All of these human foolish behaviors will bring pollution to global ocean. On consequently, we will need to compensate to eat polluted or dirty or poision fishes, ourselves bodies health will be bad. In long time, we need have high chance to pay medical expenditure when we are old. So, pollution case may be one good example to explain how and why human foolish behavior may influence ourselves future need to compensate serious medical loss.

All of these human foolish behavior will bring pollution to global ocean. On consequently, we will need to compensate to eat polluted or dirty or poison fished , ourselves bodies health will be bad. In long time, we will have high chance to pay medical expenditure, when we are old. So, pollution case may be one good example to explain how and why human ourselves intellectual or foolish behaviors may influence future long time economic loss or economic growth or recession in micro and micro economic view.

On another water pollution aspect hand, if we often keep rubbish to sea, oil exploration processing pollutes ocean and ships' gas pollute ocean, then fishes will eat polluted food and drink dirty water, due to fishes will eat polluted food and drink dirty sea water because the global ocean is polluted seriously.

In fact, because human only consider how to buy boats to carry on any leisure water activities, or catches cruises to travel on the sea. Also, oil manufacturers only consider any where to find oil exploratin places to manufacture oil products from ocean, when their pol exploration processes can plooute ocean. Consequently, global fishes drink polluted water or eat direty food. They will have poison. So, human will have high chance to eat poison fishes.

Otherwise, such as pollutin case, it can infuence inflation or deflation. Consequently, the reason indicates supply and demand theory. If air pollution is serious, then we will consider health issue, global cars demand number may be influenced to reduce, when global cars number demand will reduce, global car prices and supply number will need to change to fall down in order to attract or persuade global car consumers choose to make car purchase decision.

Hence, global car manufacture number and car price will be influenced to reduce, due to global air pollution issue. Consequently, deflation will occur because when the country citizen usually does not spend much extra saving money to buy car expensive goods. Money value will be low. Otherwise, if global cair pollution is not serious, human considers to buy cars to enjoy driving leisure lives. So, global car demand is influenced to increase , also global car price will also influenced to increase.

Consequently, gobal human will choose to buy cars to drive. Due to we accept to spend extra saving to buy expensive car goods. Car sale price and supply may be influenced to rise up. Money value is influenced to reduce. Inflation may be influenced, due to global car consumers number increases, we would not have extra money to spend easily. Car expensive goods expenditure influences our spending habit to avoid to make car purchase decision more easily. So, human intellectual or foolish activities may bring inflation or deflation consequency in possible indirectly in macro economic view.

On conclusion, above pollution case explain that how and why human intellectual or foolish economic behaviors may bring inflation or deflation consequency as wll as economic growth or recession consequency as well as any goods demand and supply increasing or decreasing consequency. It implies that human behavior may have indirect relationship to influence any goods demand and supply number to either increase or decrease result as well as any goods price will be influenced to increase or decrease in micro and macro economic view. Hence, Human foolish behavior is depended on social enjoyment need more or material social supply more because human needs to raise enjoyment feel , so we will choose to do foolish behavior, e.g. air pollution, when many people choose to buy cars to drive to replace catch public transport. So, such as car market, it depends on car demand number more than car supply number absolutely in demand and supply view.

The relationship between social change and human behavior

Why does economic changes may influence human individual behavioral change? I shall attempt to indicate shopping behavior and staying at home behavior to explain their case and effect relationsip as below:
Human behavior can be influenced by economic change or economic change can be influenced by human behavior? Why does recession may influence consumers reduce shopping desire? In social recession suitation, it is possible that many people lose jobs suddenly, due to businessmen lose many customers. They need to make decision to reduce employees number in order to continue to keep businesses. Consequently, many firms (organizations) their employees may lose jobs. When they have much time, due to lose jobs, they will feel to avoid to spend too much time and money to go to shopping often. Many losing jobs people, they will often stay at homes. So, they will reduce time to go to shopping, then non essential products won't their preferable choice purchase products. Hence, recession will change many losing jobs people their shopping or consumption desires to avoid to buy non essential products often . Usually when economic boom, many people have jobs to do because consumers number must increase when many people have jobs to do. Then, many people can accept to spend money to buy non essential products often. Many people feel spend time to go to shopping can satisfy their purchase of any kinds of new products useful psychology or desire. So, recession is one good example to explain it can influence many people do not like often to leave homes to go to shopping easily. Many people like to stay at homes, becaue they feel worry about spending too much shopping time when they leave homes. Their staying home time is one good negative shopping behavior example. So, economic change may influence human individual behavior changes , they have direct cause and efect relationship in behavioral economic view.
May human behavior influence economic change? Is it possible that human behavior may bring the country social economic change in macro economic or micro behavioral economic view ? I shall indicate publishing industry example. Do you feel that if there are many students feel learning is very important when they read many books or many of students feel interesting

to read or they have reading new books in habit, then it is possible that the country will have many students like to spend time to go to any book shops to choose the books, they feel that they can help they learn new knowledge. Then the country will increase students number, they often spend time to visit any one book shop every week. Their visiting book shops behavior which may become their habits. So, the country will increase students number, they often spend time to visit book shops. Also, it implies that visiting book shops behaviors may be their behavioral habits.

So, when the country has many students often spend time to visit book shops , their visiting book shops behaviors may help any one book shop to raise books sale chance. So, the country's student individual often visiting book shop behaviors, their habitual visiting book shops behaviors must may assist help any one book shop to increase books sale number absolutely.

Consequently, any one book shop , its books sale bumber must be influenced to increase to increase because the country will have many students like or feel need visit book shops habit in order to choose any suitable books to buy to read at home in order to raise themselves learning effort. When the country has many bok shops often have many students visit their book shops, then their books sale number may be influenced to increase. It explain why student individual visiting book shop behavior may help any one book shop sale number increases also. So, visiting shops products sale number is depended on online products supply number, if online products supply number increases, then it may cause many customers choose to buy the kind of products from online webstore. So, any shop products sale number will depend on onlint products supply number in supply and demand view.

CHAPTER FOUR

HUMAN INTELLECTUAL DEMAND AND SUPPLY BEHAVIOR RELATIONSHIP

How human productive behavior may influence economic development

May any country which citizen behavior assist themselves country development? It is one cause and effect economic question. I mean that if the country itself citicen can not concentrate mind or energy to choose to do one kind of industry in order to let themselves country can bring the most benefit, then whether the counry itself economy can bring the most serious economic benefit. I shall attempt to indicate these countries themselves indistry choice to explain whether these countries themselves citizen productive behavior may help themselves countries to achieve the largest economic benefits. I shall indicate as below:

New Zealand farmer individual wine productive behavior

For New Zealand country example, this country concerns itself effort is foucs on farming agricultural aspect. So, this country has many farmers concentrate on farming agricultural aspect. May New Zealanders choose to spend time to produce different kinds of wines, e.g. wine or red grape wine is for the people are eating meat, or they are eating dinner.

When these New Zealanders their behaviors choose to do farming or agriculture to grow and produce different kinds of taste of white or red grape wine drinking products job. Themselves grape agriculture behavior will influence these New Zealanders themselves, they can learn how to improve different kinds of grape wine drinking products in order to achieve every kinds of white or read grape wines taste improving aim during their white or red grape producing process.

Why can New Zealander every individual white or read grape wine producers improve their white or read grape wine taste more easily? In behavioral economic view, it can explain that why any one New Zealander white or read grape wine producer can be encouraged or excited or persuaded to concentrate nervous and energy and effort to learn how to improve their white or red grape wine products easily.

In fact, New Zealand is one agricultural food export country. It has good natural environment resource , e.g. land, seed to provide any one farmer to produce themselves any kinds of agricultrual food products, e.g. fruit, or wine food products. Because New Zealanders know themselves country has enough natural resource . So, in common, many New Zealanders choose to attempt to do farming agricultural jobs in order to export themselves any kinds of fruit or meat or wine products to overseas or sell to domestic in order to earn profit.

So, when these New Zealand farmers number has been increasing every year. This country farmers will feel themsleves competition between this New Zealand farmers themselves are serious due to they may feel New Zealanders choose to do agriculture businesses in order to export themselves different kinds of farming food to overseas or sell to local to earn profit.

Hence, when many New Zealand farmers feel that farmers number has been increasing every year. They will feel themselves competition is serious. They must need to spend much time and nervous and effort to research what method is the best how to produce the best taste of white or red grape wine products in order to let local or overseas wine buyers to choose to buy his/her producing white or read grpae products to drink.

Hence, in competition psychological view, may influence many New Zealand white or reaad wine producers had been beginning to change their learning behavior on researching what method is the best in order to produce the best quality of taste red or white wine products to sell in order to attract overseas or local white or read grape wine drinkers to choose to buy his/her wine products. Their behavior will focus on learning how to raising or improving white or read grape wine taste method more than only focus on producing a large number white or red grape wine products. They believe wine quality is more important to compare wine producing number. So, New Zealand wine producers themselves wine producers behaviors have been changing on concentrating on researching wine quality method aspect more then wine producing number aspect in behavioral economic view.

America high technological productive behavior

For America example, US is one high technological country, it owns many high technological knowledge talent inventors, e.g. computer science inventors. Hence, US must attract many diferent countries owning high technological computer inventors choose to go to US to develop their computer science profession career. Also, it seems that when many computer science inventors or professions choose to go to US to develop themselves computer science new career. In behavioral economic view, due to their leaving themselves countries choice, which may bring influence themselve country job behaviors need to be changed. They must need to adapt US new live. Because they will forgive their past computer science job. These computer science professionals need to spend time to adapt US new lives. They " past computer science job behaviors" will need to be changed to their new US any computer employer's new computer science job model.

Because their traditional computer science jobs needed to be forgot in their themselves countries. They will feel their old computer science job knowledge and behavior needed to change in order to let their US any one new of computer company employer feels satisfactory to accept their new working behavior in any one US computer organization.

So, on the other hand, many US computer company employer will feel that they must need time to accept any one new overseas computer science professions their working behaviors, their working attitude daily, because these foreign comouter science professional, their past computer working behaviors and working attitude must be different to US domestic computer science professions.

In behavioral economic view, these overseas computer science professions, their working behaviors and attitude must be needed to change in order to adapt any one US new computer company itself domestic or local computer science professional stafs themselves daily working behaviors and attitude because these overseas and local computer science professionals must need to team work together.

In behavioral economic view, it is only one way that foreign computer science professionals must need to change themselves past country traditiona daily working behaviors and attitude in order to cooperate with these US local computer science professionals in teams more easily.

Consequently, if these foreign compute science professionals can change their past working behaviors and attitude to let any one US local computer science professional feels to cooperate with them easily in short time. Then, the US computer company itself whole computer professional teams themselves efficiencies will be influenced to raised or improved by the changing past working attitude and working behaviors of these foreign computer science professionals. So, in behavioral economic view, only if US any one computer company hopes itself computer teams themselves efficiency can be raised or improved when it decides to employ foreign computer science professionals and US domestic computer science professionals. They need to work in teams together. They must need to let these foreign computer science professionals to know how to change their working behaviors and attitude to let their domestic computer science professionals feel easy to work together. Then, the US computer company itself whole team efficiency must be rasied or improved easily in short time.

- China share market investing behavior

For China share market example, economic development depends on financial market. Because if many Chinese have interest to invest to carry on shares buying and selling activities in orde to learn how to earn shares interest and share profit when the China shareholder can make decision to sell himself/herself shares in the the high price, then he/she can earn money when he/she can sell the China company's shares in the high sale share price position.

If China has many Chinese like to spend time to carry on investing shares activities. Themselves shares buying and selling behaviors will influence China has many companies can increase fund from many Chinese shareholders in order to have enough money to expand or develop themselves businesses in China in long term.

Consequently, when China can have many Chinese like to attempt to carry on buying and selling shares investing behaviors in China share market. Themselves buying and selling shares behaviors can help many Chinese companies have effort to increase enough money or capital in order to continue to do their businesses in long term absolutely. So, it explains why when many Chinese become shareholders , they can assist China will have many companies continue to develop their businesses if many Chinese like to carry on shares buying and selling investing behaviors in long time in China financial investment market nowadays in behavioral economic view.

Why has any individual country have many people invest share behavior which can influence the country's macro consumption desire?

I shall apply shares market buying and selling investment behavior to explaiin why shares investment behavior which may impact the country's overal consumption desire as below:

In behavioral economic view, I assume that when the coutry has many people have interest to attempt to carry on shares buying and selling investment behavior, then their frequent shares buying and selling behaviors which may bring negactive consumption desire or shopping desire of these shares investors their consumer behavior.

The reason is simple, when the country has many share buyers number suddenly been increasing rapidly. Consequently, these large group share investors must need to spend much time to research any kinds of company shares variations, whether when their share prices will rise up of fall down in order to achieve buying the company's shares in the lowest price and selling the company's shares in the highest price level in order to earn profit.

Basic on this reason, they must need to spend much extra time to research share prices changing behavior every day, e.g. one working person will wait to leave his/her job, after he/she can spend time to gather data to research the day's share price changing behavior after dinner. So, the working person's right time may be his/her share price market research behavior. Before he/she may spend his/her night time to go to shopping after dinner, but nowadays, he/she will fogive to do his/her shopping behavior before dinner or after dinner at hight sometime. He/she will make decision to spend much night time to turn on computer to click on share market website to research his/her share purchase choice to investigate whether his/her share price whether it rises up or falls down at the moment in order to make his/her share buying or selling decision at ever night time.

I mean the when the country has many people are share investors, their shares investment behavioral spenging time which will influence many shops lose customers at might often because the country will have many people feel need to spend night time to turn on computer or watch television to investigate share price variation. So, the country will have many people / share investors choose to stay at home in order to carry on share price variation investigation behavior, they need to listen share market update news from radios or watch the share market update news from computer or TV at home every night. Consequenly, they must reduce times to leave themselves homes at night. So, their shopping behavior also will be reduced. Because these share investors feel need to spend time to investigate share price variation news at homes which can bring economic benefits (high opportunity benefits) when they choose to forgive to leave homes to go to shopping times (opportunity cost) every night.

On conclusion, it seems that when the country has many people are share investors, then their share price investigating behavior may bring negative shopping emotion at night. Consequently, the country's any one shop may lose many customers from this share investor consumer group in behavioral economic view. Hence, when the country's share investors number had been increasing rapidly, it will influence any shops lose many customers from this share investing customer group at night frequenly in short time, even long time in behavioral economic view, because their shopping desires or shopping emotion will be brought negative feeling when they make decisions to spend much time to listen radios or watch TV or computers share price update nes at night. Hence, share market will bring negative impact to influence consumer shopping desire or negative shopping emotion in behavioral economic view.

CHAPTER FIVE

TECHNOLOGY DEMAND AND SUPPLY RELATIONSHIP

Can technology influence human shopping behavioral change?
Nowadays, technological development has reached mature stage, whether technological mature stage may bring positive or negative shopping emotion influence to global consumers. I shall aplly internet inventin or ecommerce shopping channel tool to explain whether internet technology can bring postive or negative influence to global consumer behavior in behavioral economic view.

Internet is a good technological tool, it brings e-commerce business chance. In fact, commonly, global has have many businessmen choose to use internet channel to carry on their products transactions between global online-buyers and their electronic websites. So, global many shoppers had begun to feel online shopping is more convenient to compare visiting shops shopping. Their shopping behaviors have been changed from internet technological tool. Global has many shoppers choose to buy any products from any overseas or local businessmen their web stores. They only need to spend time to find any businessmen their webstores to choose the most suitable products to pay visa to buy from their webstores. at homes. So, in general, global had have may shoppers had changed their shopping behaviors from visiting shops to visiting webstores at homes often.

So, it seems that internet technological tool had influenced global many shops disappear, but internet webstores will be replaced their actual shops on streets. Some of businessmen either they choose webstores to replace shops or choose websotes and shops both or still keep shops only. Hence, internet tool influences global businessmen have three kinds of products sale channels to let globa local and overseas consumers to choose how to buy their products.

However, in fact, many of global shoppers, youngers and olders had begun to accept to buy any products from webstores. They feel to spend time to leave homes to visit shops , their shopping behaviors will be wasted time to not essential part to their daily lives. Hence, since internet technological invention, it had changed many consumers their traditional visiting shops shopping habit to change to buying products from webstores channel.

However, on the one hand, internet creates webstores ecommerce shopping channel to let global many consumers do not need to leave homes to go to shopping. It brings negative visiting shops shopping emotion to global general consumers nowadays. But on the other hand, it also brings positive visiting internet webstores shopping emotion to global general consumer nowadays. So, it seems that global many consumers feel that they often do not need to spend much time to go out shopping. Many global consumers feel convenient and enjoy to choose any products to buy from different internet webstores, when the online buyer chooses the most suitable product, he she only needs to pay visa card to buy the product from the online seller's webstore conveniently at home.

Hence, online shopping can bring economic benefit to online buyers, e.g. avoiding walking time or spending transport fare to visit the shop to go to shopping, shortening or reducing shopping time to do another important matter.

On conclusion, global many consumers began feel online shopping can bring more economic benefits on shortening shopping time, avoiding transport fare spending aspect. So, online shopping will be popular shopping behavior for future long time. It may encourage global many shoppers can make rapid shopping decision in short time in order to carry on any products buying transaction to global any one online shopper in short time easily in behavioral economic view. So, global many businessmen had begun to build themselves one attraction webstore in order to persuade different countries consumers to choose to click themselves webstores from internet channel to buy any kinds of products in short time easily.

So, internet technology had changed consumers traditional shopping behaviors to build positive online shopping emotion as well as raise online sellers' any products sale chance easily in behavioral economic view.

Why and how human behavior may influence the country's economic growth or recession?

When one country has many people choose to do the same matter for one period, whether their behavior may influence the country's pvera; economic growth or recession . I shall attempt to indicate cases toexplain their relationship as below:

For flowing rubblish behavioral case example, do you feel that when the country has many people often flow rubblish on the streets, instead of their flowing rubblish behavior may bring streets dirty? But, their flowing rubblish behavior may explain that this country has people may have enough money to buy food to ear, or enough cloths to wear, enough bottles of water to drink, even they may have enough money to buy new television, radio, refrigeraters , washing machines, desktops or laptops electronic home products from old to new to use in order to satisfy their living needs. So, when they flow old electronic home products, their flowing old home electronic products behaviors may seem that they have enough money to buy other new home electronic products to replace old home electronic products to use at homes.

However, it seems thaat this country ought have many people have jobs to do. So, many of them, they can easy to make purchase decison to flow any old home electronic products and buy any new home electronic products to use . Because this country has many people have jobs to do. So, they can often not use old home electonic products to become rubblishs to flow on streets after they had bought any kinds of new home electronic homes.

In fact, it also implies that this country's economy grows rapidly. So, many businesses can glow up rapdly. When they expanded their businesses, they must need to increase employees number in order to let they help themselves to raise productivity or serve their clients absolutely. So, when the country has many businesses can grow up, it seems that its economy must be better or it is improved to compare past. Due to many different kinds of home electronic products had been often bought to use by this country people in this period. So, this country's any streets can be observed that expensive electronic home products were flowed on streets anywhere. then, this country will have many electronic home products sellers can sell their home electronic products very easily. When this country has many people can find any kinds of jobs to do easily. So, due to unemploymen rate had been decreasing.

In behavioral economic view, as this many electronic home products rubblish country case, we can observe this country may have many people have jobs to do. So, consumption number has been increased long time. So, cheap food, or expensive home electronic products may be rubblish on any streets. This country's people , their flowing rubblish behaviors may be explained that many of people have enough jobs to do, so they have ability to buy any good taste food to eat or buy any kinds of expensive electronic home products to use. So, this country's economy may be improved for this long period. So, in behavioral economic view, when this country can have many electronic home products rubblishs are flowed on anywherer in streets frequently. It seems that this country will have many people have jobs to do, so it causes they often change old home electronic products or replaced them easily, when they have enough income to spend to buy any kinds of new home electronic products to use at homes easily. Moreover, their flowing old electronic home products behaviors also indicate that this country has many people their salaries may be increased in possible from their emplyers. When this country can have many different kinds of home electornic products are sold. It means that this country's electronic home products needs or demand had been increasing, due to many people have jobs to do and income increases to excite their living of needs also improve. Consequently, this country may seem have better economic improvement. We can observe from this country's electronic home products rubblish increasing income in theis period.

On conclusion, this country ought experience economic growth at this period. So, " flowing expensive electronic home rubblish increasing number " may seem that this country's economic growth is rapidly in this period, due to many people have jobs to do as well as salaries increase in this period.

Technology how impacts human behavior changing?

Technology how influences human behavior to bring changing? For example, online share purchase and sale transaction from smart phone brings share investor can do share buying or selling transation in any where and any time conveniently, non manual driving auto vehicle, bring car owner feels comfortable and spends free time to do other matter, e.g. reading, listening mucis in himself or herself car freely. electrical energy vehicle can help car owner to reduce air polluton and it can brings the drivers do not feel drive long time in any journeys in order to avoid air pollution for environmental protection responsible car drivers in our societies. Thus, they will drive long time in any journeys when they can drive electronic energy cars to replace oil energy cars.

However, online technology can also bring consumers can choose to stay at homes to buy any things from seller individual online webstore conveniently. Such as online technology can bring shoppers do not need to spend much time to visit shops to buy any things. They can choose any kinds of products from any online sellers individual online webstores conveniently at homes. Online technology excite busy consumers can make purchase decision easily as well as it can help online sellers sell any kinds of products from internet easily.

In behavioral economic view, technology can change human behavior to be improved, it can let human feels comfortable, more free time ro use, rapid making any decisions, such as apply smart phones to make share purchase or sale transaction decision, online shopping decision, even travelling any where decision in short time, when the traveller finds the most cheap hotel accommodation room price and air ticket price frm any travel agent online tourism webstore, then the potential travel customer can follow the online hotel accommodation price and air ticket price data to make decision when to buy the air ticket from the airline travel agent or make decision when to prebook which hotel accommodation room to go to the country to travel from online travel agent tourism webstores. So, technology can encourage global any country travelers to make anywhere to trvel rapidly. If the traveler can find the country's general hotel rooms and airline tickets prices had been decreasing more sightly. The traveler may make travel decision to choose the country to travel in short time, then he/she can prebook the country;s any hotel room and airline ticket to pay by visa fraom the country's any hotel and airline travel agent webstores., before one week, even one month or more easily. Hence, online technology can also encourage traveler individual frequent travel times to be increased, due to global travelers can find any hotel rooms and airline tickets prices from internet conveniently at homes. They do not need to spend time to visit any airline travel agent to enquire travel choice country's hotel rooms prices and airline ticket prices. They can compare global travel of countries choices ' all hotels rooms and airline agents air tickets prices to make prebook airline seat and hotel room decision before one week, one month even six months early.

On conclusion, online technology can encourage global travelers can make travelling any where and when traveling time desicions easily. It can excite tourism industry develops in long time. Also, such as electricity cars invention can encourage environment protection car owners do car purchase decision easily, because they can choose to drive electronic energy cars to replace oil energy cars in order to avoid air pollution occurs easily. So, electronic cars can increase electronic car purchasrs number, due to many of environmental protection attitude of car owners can choose to drive electricity cars to bring air cleans, even non -manual driving cars can encourage lazy driving and free time driving car owners to choose to buy non-manual (artificial intelligent) cars to drive , because they can spend much free time to read, listen music or do any matters in themselves cars, they do not need to drive cars, robotic (AI) auto driving machine is such one non-manual driver to help them to drive themselves cars confidently. So, non-manual driving cars can attract lazy and enjoying free time driving car owners to choose to buy to replace traditional manual cars to drive easily. Moreover, online share transaction can help any share investors to make share buying and selling decision in short time easily. When they can apply smart phones technological tool to carry on share buying and selling activities easily. They can observe any share rising or falling price suitation from smart phones in any where any any time easily. So, smart phone technology can help global any shareholders to make share purchase and sale transaction easily. So, technology can encourage human makes decision in short time rapidly.

How and why employees behaviors may influence economy development?

In behavioral economy view,I believe the country's any organizational employees behavior may bring indirect relationship to influence the country's long term economic development. I shall indicate past manufacture industry social development period to explain their relationship. For many countries‘ past business activities had belonged to manufacturing industry, such as US, UK past before 1980 year, it focused on steel manufacturing and steel manufacturing related machine products. So, US, Uk developed countries manufacturing industries may be past main country's economic income sources. I assume US , UK past had one million number different kinds of industries. They ought had about seven houndred thousand number organizational businesses were belonged to manufactured industry. They may include:

Steel manufacturing and steel related machine manufacturing, e.g. vehicle manufacturing, home appliances, e.g. washing machine, television, radio, refrigerate cooler, heater, air condition etc. different kinds of different kinds of steel -related manufacturing machine, they were manufactured from US, UK steel machine manufacturers. So, US, Uk the other three hundred thousand number industry may be general service industry, e.g. hotel service, restaurent, cinema, public transport service, tourism lesiure , wine bar, supermarket etc. different kinds of non-manufacturing industries business organizations were operated in UK, US past before 1980 year.

So, in UK, US developed countries industry development history, they ought have high percentage of businesses belonged to steel related manufacturing machine and steel products. Also, in the past before 1980 year, US, Uk business employers , they employed many workers are manufacturing workers. They needed to spend long time to work in factories. They were skillful workers, and they are trained to manufacturing cars, washing machine, television, heater, etc. even steel itself different kinds of steel related products to prepare to deliver to their shops to sell to US, Uk local or overseas clients.

So, I believe that past UK, US ought employ many employees, they belonged to skillful manufacturing workers, manufacture increasing steel machine or steel related machine number of products rapidly daily. So, if UK, US had had many of these manufacturing factories owned high skillful workers, then their manufacturing steel-related machine or steel both kinds of products number must be influenced to raise rapidly. Consequently, their steel machine manufacturing products would been exported to overseas or would been sold to local both markets , they may be influenced to raise sale number. They (these manufacturing workers) needed to be trained to know how to manufactur these different kinds of machine products in the efficient teams and they ought to be trained to raise their efficiencies in order to shorten time to manufacturing many kinds of steel related manufacturing machine or steel itself products rapidly. So , if their efficiencies and manufacturing performance was improved, these US, UK any one manufacturing worker and their teams ought achieve raising productivities significantly.

Hence, when past UK, US manufacturing industry development period, if these two countries' any manufacturing factories could have many manufacturing workers could be trained to be skillful and proficient manufacturing workers. Then, in past every day to these factories workers, they ought help their steel or steel related manufacturing employers to raise any kinds of machine or steel products number in every team. So, when past in the manufacturing industry development, US, UK could have many factories' manufacturing workers themselves steel or steel related machine products manufacturing skill could be trained to to improve to any kinds of these machine or steel manufacuring products quality as well as their products number could be influenced to raise by themselves skillful improvement significantly every day.

Then, what would be influenced to occur to past UK, US manufacturing industry period? In behavioral economic view, when these two manufacturing industry developed countries, such as UK, US , if they had many factories workers can be trained to improve their skill in order to achieve any kinds of steel or steel-related machine products quality could be improved as well as products manufacturing number could be also increased absolutely.

In consequence, past UK and US both countries ought increase themselves any kinds of steel and steel related machine products number to be supplied to themselves local shops to let local clients to choose any one kind of machine manufacturing products to buy easily as well as they could also export to supply overseas any countries to buy their different kinds of steel or steel related machine products to let overseas steel or steel related manufacturing machine product buyers, they can have many of these different kinds of these steel or steel-related different kinds of manufacturing machine from UK and UK these both countries easily to compare other countries.

On conclusion, I believe that past US, and UK macro manufacturing industry income GDP would increase significantly. So, they would have good economic growth performance because when many of these manufacturing workers themselves manufacturing effort could be improved. So, it explained when employees manufacturing abilities can influence economic growth indirectly.

Robots invention whether they can help organizations to raise efficiencies or inefficiencies?

In behavioral economic view, in any organizations, when the organization hopes its worker teams can raise efficiencies , the organization may choose to increase more workers number and/or it can provide training to improve these workets themselves skills in order to raise their efficiencies. For one warehouse example, when the warehouse increases many goods , they are needed to delivered these goods from the shelves to the delivering destination locations. If this warehouse supervisors feel these workers themselves goods delivery speeds are slow, which is possible due to this warehouse's workers number is not enough. So, this warehouse supervisor ought increase workers number in order to increase their goods delivery speed in order to deliver goods from the shelves to every indicated goods delivery destination in order to let any one lorry driver can transport the right kinds of goods and ensure the accurate goods number to transport to any one client home rapidly.

However, if this warehouse supervisor planed to buy several warehouse goods delivery robots to assist these warehouse workers to find the right kinds of goods from shelves and then deliver to the right destination location in the warehouse. So, these warehouse orkers can concentrate on counting the accurate goods number and ensuring the right kinds of goods in order to prepare to let lorry drivers to transport these goods to these goods of buyers themselvers homes rapidly. Consequently, in the first step, robots can concentrate on finding th right goods from shelves and delivers them to the right goods transportation of location destination. Then, in the second step, these warehouse workers can concentrate on counting the accurate goods number and ensuring the right kinds of goods in order to prepare to put them to the lorry. Consequently, when warehouse robots and warehouse workers can cooperate to work together, the most important, robots, can deal on finding the right kinds of goods and deal on delivering the accurate number of goods of job duty as well as these warehouse workers can only concentrte on counting the right kinds of goods number in order to avoid it has none any mistake of wrong kinds of goods and inaccurate goods of delivery number to be transported to the lorry and to deliver to any one buyer's home.

So, it seems that warehouse robots ought help any one warehouse worker to raise himself efficiency and avoid goods delivery of mistake occurrence easily as well as their help to warehouse workers that can let any one goods buyer feels their goods can be delivered to their homes rapidly. Moreover, warehouse robots can also help these warehouse workers to raise efficiencies because warehouse robots can help them to shorten goods delivery time between any one shelf and any one goods delivery destination of location in the warehuse because robots may help them to find the right kinds of goods from the right shelf in the short time. So, any one worker does not need to spend long time to seek anywhere is the right shelf location for the kind of goods when the kind of goods are needed to deliver to the buyer's home from lorry. Warehouse robots can help them to do this aspect of " finding the goods from the right shelf in short time job duty". So, any one warehouse worker only needed tospend less time to do the counting of any right kind of goods number and ensuring the right kind of goods job duty. Consequently, this warehouse 's any one worker, his any one kind of goods delivery time may be reduced, because robots' assistance and they may have more confidence to avoid mistake to deliver the wrong number of goods and/or the wrong kind of goods to any one goods buyer's home.

On conclusion, it seems that warehouse robots ought may help any one warehouse worker to raise efficiency for any one team in the warehouse as well as the warehouse any one supervisor does not need to spend much time to observe any one worker individual performance for " goods delivery job duty aspect" because their goods delivery job duty that had been replaced to do by these several warehouse robots. Robots can achieve the more accurate of right kinds of goods and the right number of goods delviery job performance to compare any one of human warehouse worker themselves right kinds of goods of delivery and right number of goods of delivery job performance. So, when robots can participate to cooperate with this warehouse's any one worker to do their goods of delivery job duty in this warehouse every day. Then, robots can raies any one of supervisor individual confidence in order to let they do not need to spend time to observe any one of worker individual whose goods of delivery job performane. They can concentrate on supervising any one worker whose goods transport to lorry in the final step in order to avoid to deliver wrong goods number and / or wrong kind of goods to any one goods buyer's home every day. Consequently, this warehouse's overall teams of their delviery of goods performance many be improved by robotss‘ participatin to goods of delivery task as well as this warehouse's oveall teams themselves efficiencies may be influenced to raise by robots' goods of delivery task participation.

Why social behavior may influence organizational strategy needs to be changed ?

Why any organizations need to know whether nowadays social behaivor how has been changing in order to implement the kind of the most right strategy to achieve the profit aim pursue in possible. I shall indicate nowadays ecommerce or online, customer shopping behavior to explain above question concerns they ought have close relationship between social behavior and organizational strategic choice or organizational behavioral changing need.

On nowadays ecommerce business, or online shopping model, this kind of shopping model in global many young and old age consumers like to apply internet tool to choose any country sellers website stores in order to stay at home to buy any kinds of products from themselves webstores in global societies.
In fact, online shopping model had been popular for long time above to twenty years. Most of global sellers will make decision to design themselves webstores in order to attract global many online buyers to choose to buy their products from themselves webstores. So, it seems that social consumers purchase behaviors had been changed to online shopping from internet invention.
Hence, social consumers purchase behavioral changes may influence any organizations‘ strategies need to be changed from visiting shops purchase strategy model to online purchase strategy model, if the seller still concentrate on concentrate on considerate how to design itelf , but neglects to considerate how to design itself webstore, e.g. how to design attract product photos to put on itself webstore, how to arrange sale price information location to be putted on webstore and visa card payment location on itself webstore in order to let any one online buyer can feel very easier to buy itself any kinds of products from itself webstore. Then, its potential online buyers will be influenced to increase number when they can find this online seller itself any kinds of products photes and every kinds of product sale price information and visa card payment channel locations easily from itself webstore.
So, it implies that nowadays any one seller ought need to design one webstore to let any one online overseas and domestic consumers can have chance to click itself webstore to choose any one kind of product to buy conveniently when he/she does not hope to leave him/her home to go to shop, because nowadays social shopping behaviors had been influenced to change when internet invention, them it gives another online purchase method to replace visiting shops purchase method to global any one buyer in nowadays societies.
So, if nowadays any one seller still concentrate on how to design itself shop display in order to put any kinds of product on shelf in order to let any one visiting shop customer to find the kind of product to buy, but it neglects to change to choose to pursue another new technological shopping method, such as webstore purchase method in order to implement effective strategy to design the most right webstore as well as in order to attract global

overseas and local consumers to find itself webstore easily from website and find its any one kind of product phots and sale price and visa card payment button in order to choose to buy itself any kinds of products in the short time. Consequently I believe that the seller will lose many customers from overseas and local when its other same or similar product sellers choose to design themselves webstores in order to let global any one product buyer can buy themselves any one kind of product when they can pay visa card to buy their products from them webstores conveniently when they stay at home habitly. Then, the seller will lose many global potential customers in long time.

On conclusion, in behavioral economic view, any consumer behavioral social changing, which will influence any in order to avoid customers number loses significantly . In future time, organizations need to make rapid decision in order to implement the most reasonable and the most useful strategy in order to avoid global potential customers number reduces or lose them in long time. So, social behavioral changing environment ought influence any global organizations need to decide how to change themselves strategies in order to avoid customers loses significantly in future time.

How and why human behavior may influence economic growth or recession?

May ourselves daily behaviors influence our global societial continue economic growth or recession? Do they have cause and effect close relationship between human behaviors and global economic growth or recession? I shall apply behavioral economic theory to analyze and explain whether ourselves daily behaviors and our global societial economic growth or recession which have close cause and effect relationship as below:

Every country itself economic development must depend on any business activities, otherwise, any kinds of business activities must need ourselves business activities or behaviors in order to achieve any business activities as well as achieve the country's overall economic development in macro view. However, any country's overall business activites or behaviors which must depend on any kinds of individual businessmen, themselves employees daily working behavior or activity or performance in order to help them to attract or increase many clients number to acieve " earning profit" aim. So, it seems that any individual business, itself overall every department individual working behavior is one main factor to influence the company's overall business performance.

For agricultural fruit and meat food farming industry example, such as New Zealand is a farming main target industry country. It had had many New Zealanders were daily themselves own farming businesses for many years. Their farming businesses include growing fruit, sheep, cow, pig pork, meat etc. food sale business. If the New Zealand farmer owned a large size farming land, then he will choose either growing fruit or feeding sheeps, pigs, cows to be meat to to transport to New Zealand supermarkets to help them to sell to their farmers meet to New Zealanders in order to earn profit. Thus, if the New Zealand farmer owned large size of farming lands, then he needs to employ many farming employees (farming workers) to help him to carry on farming business daily tasks, e.g. picking up friuts, feeding pigs, cows, sheeps to eat food daily. These daily farming jobs are very important to influence this New Zealand farmer's meats or fruits sale number whether they can be easy or diffcult to sell in New Zealand supermarkets , if these farming workers can own encough farming knowledge or skill to know how to pick up fruits method and make judgement to know whether it is right time to pick up the kind of fruits from the trees , as well as know how feed this pigs, sheeps, cows to eat food in order to let they are better health. Consequently, their farming behaviors which can let these animals can provide the best taste and enough meat from these animals to let New Zealander to buy to eat from New Zealand any one supermarket. Even these New Zealand farming workers can know whether the kinds of fruits, e.g. oranges, apples, gapes etc. fruits whether they ought be picked up from the trees at the right time. Consequently, they can make judgement to decide to pick up any kinds of the best taste fruits to let any one New Zealander to buy to eat from any one supermarket in New Zealand. Otherwise, if they do not make judegement to know whether the kind of fruit ought not be picked up because they still need longer time to continue grow up to increase fruit size and better taste from the trees in order to let any one fruit buyer can feel better taste when they eat this kind of fruit later. If they can buy this kind of fruit to eat later, then this New Zealand farmer's his fruit buyers can buy the best taste of this kind of fruit to eat from an yone supermarket in New Zealand. Consequently, many New Zealand supermarkets will choose to buy any kinds of fruits from this farmer fruit supplier when they feel this farmer's fruits can provide more better taste fruits to compare other farmers' fruits.

Thus, due to New Zealand is one farming main income source country. It's any kinds of fruits and meats need to be export to overseas to sell , instead of local sale. It's GDP percent is very high to whole country 's overall income source. So, any one New Zealand farmer individual and any one farming worker individual working behavior will influence its economy whether it is influenced to grow or recession possible. Moreover, it also seems that farming workers' farming knowledge and skill will influence themselves farming daily activities to achieve the aim of the number of increase or decrease to any kinds of fruits whether they are better taste or the number of increase of decrease to any kinds of meats whether they are better taste to supply to any one New Zealand fruit or meat buyers to eat from any one New Zealand supermarket. So, it implies that any one New Zealand farming worker individual farming behavior may influence any kinds of fruits or any kinds of meat taste because they are transported to any one supermarket to sell in New Zealand.

Consequently, if New Zealans had many farmers can teach god farming knowledge and skill to let their any one farming workers know how to decide judgement to decide when it is right time to pick up any kinds of fruits from trees , or how to grow them on soil in order to let they can grow rapidly. Then, many different kinds of fruits can be provided to let any one New Zealanders can eat the best taste of fruits when their fruits are supplied to any one New Zealand supermarkets. Even, if they knew how to feed foods to pigs, cows, sheeps to eat daily. Then they can be more health and they can provide the best taste of meats to let any one New Zealanders can buy their meats from any one New Zealand supermarkets. Moreover, their fruits and meats can be transported to overseas to let any one country fruits or meats buyers can choose any kinds of New Zealand meats and fruits to buy to eat from themselves countries supermarkets. Then, many overseas fruit and meat buyers will perfer to choose New Zealand any kinds of fruits or meats to buy to compare other countries fruits or meats to buy when they go to any one local supermarkets.

On conclusion, it seems that New Zealand farming workers themselves farming behavior may influence their farming employers any kinds of fruits or meats sale number and income because their farming task behaviors must influence whether their fruits or meats taste are the better taste or worse taste to compare their other local farmers (the farmer competitors) whose fruits or meats taste. If tthe farmer's any one farming worker can be trained to learn how to know to feed animals skill and when is the most right time to pick up any kinds of fruits from trees or how to grow them on the soil methods. Due to these farming worker individual farming behavior may influence his different finds of fruits and meats sale number to be increase or decrease, so these any one New Zealand farmer must need to depend on any one farming worker whose farming working methods, if their farming working behaviors can be the best to influence any kinds of fruits to grow rapid or any kinds of pigs, cows, sheeps animals grow up rapidly , then their sale number may be increase significantly and their taste can be improved to let any New Zealand or overseas meat or fruit buyer to buy to eat to feel from any one New Zealand or overseas supermarkets, then New Zealand's agriculture industry must be influenced to increase. In the world, any one fruit or meat buyer must choose to buy New Zealand's fruit and meat to eat in prefer to compare other countries' fruits and meats. So, New Zealand's GDP may be influenced to raise from any one New Zealand farming worker individual farming working behaviors. It seems that New Zealand farmer fruit and meat sale number is depended on their eatting consumers demand more than their meat and fruit supply because if these NZ farmers can apply high technology method to grow good taste fruit or feed good taste meat to let global eatting customers to feel, their demand will increase, then NZ farmers will need to increase good taste fruit and good taste meat supply number to satisfy global meat and fruit eatting customer taste need.

CHAPTER SIX

ILLNESS HOW INFLUENCE LEISURE ONLINE SHOPPING DEMAND AND SUPPLY CHANGES

How COVID 19 disease influences tourism leisure need

How COVID disease influences global oil need and price change to impact
travelling lesisure industry development

- The prediction of price factor influences space traveler number

The space tourism leisure organizations indicate the total cost of a trip into space is rapidly coming down from the initial price level of about US$600,000, it is obvious that the space travelling customer base is going to be rather small. Typical customers tend to belong to the top 1% income bracket. They also indicate that the price comes down , it is expected that new space travelling customer groups will enter the space tourism leisure market.

Typical new customers include people in other brackets with one-of-a kind incomes, such as inheritance or business sold. There are indications that those types of customers are becoming interested in spending on an once-in-a lifetime space experience. Therefore, the growth of the space tourism market is highly sensitive to customer satisfaction and how it is communicated through various media.

This will establish the status factors of space tourism and corresponding brand reputation service providers. They also suggest that any operator monitors space travelling customer satisfaction closely, as it will help developing increasingly accurate estimates of how the space tourism leisure market will develop.

Hence, it seems that every time space tourism journey price variable factor will influence the time space tourism of customer individual leisure desire and the space tourism passenger number. For example, the minimum price goal foe a variable space tourism business is currently estimate to be below US$3000-4000/kg for a round -trip depending on variable configuration and operation size. At this price, they estimate that somewhat over 1 % of the high income earners are potential customers.

However, for significant volume growth the longer term goal should be below US$2000/kg for a typical passenger, baggage and supplies. The lower price will probably open space tourism to a broader population, expanding the customer base and altering expectations. beyond this point space tourism will become into a travelling competitive leisure commodity, price competition will ensure and service providers need to rethink their space tourism marketing and branding and price strategies.

I shall also recommend how to attract the potential customers successfully. First, space operators need to pay special attention to the right level of customer services. Second, various preparatory customer operations cost, such as a travel to the launch site, space tourism destination accommodation, pre-flight training, medical check-ups and equipment my add up to between 10 to 15 % of the actual space travel cost. Thurs, solving the right balance between services offered and cost of client operation in order to earn the largest intangible benefits, such as loyalty, confidence, leisure enjoyment, comfortable space travelling journey as well as tangible benefits, such as profit, spacecraft manufacturing facilities, space stations, space hotels , space swimming pools, space gardens, space cinema etc. which are built to similar to earth building facilities to satisfy space travelers‘ needs.

The influential factors persuade travelers choose space tourism

Nowadays, our earth is no longer an adventurous enough place for some experienced tourists. Space tourism will be a new sector of adventure tourism, which is in the near future will be fast becoming a new tourism leisure opportunity for experiencing the unknown. Of one day, space tourism is able to reach the mass tourism phase, due to improved safety and decreased operation costs, a future space tourist will possibly only need minimal training to cope with the zero cost.

Space tourism is quite well established with visits to space attraction and launch sites, and it is a wealthy trips to the international space station for any space tourism travelers. However, if any space tourism leisure companies can attempt to find what the most influential factors are to persuade travelers feel attraction more than travelling in our earth.

It aims to let travelers to choose space travelling more than earth travelling when they feel travelling leisure need. I shall indicate what will be the most important influential factors to persuade travelers to choose space tourism more than earth tourism as below:

Firstly, I shall argue that the majority of different new space tourism journey destinations will be needed to find to satisfy different aged space travelers and different income space tourism consumers' needs. For example, the rich people have effort to consume longer time and reach any space tourism destinations where are far away from our earth of their every space tourism journey.

Otherwise, the middle income people will choose shorter space tourism journey distance from our earth and short time space tourism journey. Also, younger space tourism clients can accept more longer journey time, exciting fast speed spacecraft flying journey. Otherwise, old space tourism clients can only accept comfortable and shorter time safe space journey. So, it seems that safety, comfortable feeling, shorter time space tourism journey won't be one important influential factor to excite any young people who choose to consume space tourism leisure. Otherwise, safety, comfortable feeling, shorter time space tourism journey will be one important influential factor to excite any old people who choose to consume space tourism leisure.

Secondly, the another most important influential factor to excite space travelers to choose space tourism , it concerns whether the space travelers will feel what tourists benefits can be earned from a substantial variety of destinations choice. In general, space tourism with those of aviation, space travelers will hope space tourism will be travelling distances by air in a very short time, safely and comfortably, to bring them to arrive any space planet destinations when spacecraft reaches any space stations to stay in any space destinations.

Hence, space destination factor will bring important influential choice to any space destination journeys. As a result of the space technological tourism boom, the number of potential different space destination, choice attractions have grown with far fewer places on earth to which human do have access yet. However, the ultimate different space destinations to which many of us dream is not on earth, but as least 100 km above us, anywhere in space any planets.

If the space tourism leisure company can provide different space tourism destination choices to young or old age both space traveler target consumer groups. They will feel a real holiday when they will be able to enjoy a great image of the earth from planets. It might mean that every space tourism journey can provide different space tourism destination to let space travelers have another new travelling destinations where are far from our earth anywhere.

Hence, the different space tourism destinations will give them an unforgettable adventure. Think of how it would be to be able to check in at a " billion strategy" luxury hotel in space one planet, it means that the space planet destination can provide one luxury hotel to let space travelers to live one night or more in the space planet destination, how it would be to schedule the space traveler' vacation at one of the space tourism leisure company luxury resorts on the Moon or Mars.

This images seem from science fiction movies, but one should not forget that 100 years ago, the Wright brothers, aviation pioneers inventors and builders of the air plane, would not have imagined how, every day it is possible that future spacecraft can fly to any planets to let human have chance to stay in the space hotel one night or more.

Consequently, space destination choice and space tourism journey service performance, aviation safety, ticket price and leisure satisfactory feeling which will be important influential factors to attract future space travelers to choose space tourism leisure to replace earth tourism leisure in future one day.

How to achieve these two main space tourism objectives.

However, these are key questions continually asked regarding the viability of space tourism. They concern financial, marketing and political communities. Their concerns can be best addredded in a properly, comprehensive business plan. Some questions can not be answered definitively at this time. Hoever, knowledge of the concerns and developing space businesses in any space traveling leisure planning stages and efforts to raise capital in the following questions, every spce tourism leisure business

leader needs to concern this questions as below:
Can the space tourism industry into a profitable enonomic industry?
Are challenges related to financing, marketing, business methodologies or a combination of all of these facets?
Can the proponents of space tourism to be proven business tools and methodologies in their presentation of an acceptable business plan?
Can at least a cost effective, certified passenger space tourism journey to be developed for space tourism?
What effects will influence space-tourism businesses of NASA begins selling seats on the US space shuttle to civilian space tourists?
All above questions will be every new space tourism leisure businessman who needs to concern questions in order to achieve whose marketing strategy more successfully. Consequently, marketing strategy is important to be prepared in order to follow corrective steps to achieve every space tourism leisure business missions and objectives more easily.

● Space tourism leisure behavioral economic consumption model

In space tourism leisure industry, due to every time space trip needs the space travelling planner to plan how much budget to consume expensive spce ticket price. So, it seems that the target customers will be rich or high income level young people or the retirement rich old people target customer group.
So, it brings this question: How to persuade these rich or high income young people or rich retirement old people to prefer to spend spce tourism leisure at least one time in their life?
It is one valuabe research question to every future space tourism leisure provider. I shall indicate the successful factors to analyze how to persuade them to accept this kind of potential space travelling leisure in behavioral economic personal consumption view point, in order to explain the cause and effect relationship between of these factors as below:

(1) Economic environment variable factor

Firstly, it is economic environment variable factor whether it can influence to space tourism leisure consumption changing. As I discuss about economic environment variable issue will influence consumption behavior changing. For space tourism leisure case, it is not now kind of essential consumption leisure product to every one. So , even the rich or high income people who will be influences to seek this kind of leisure to play, it the economic environment is improved, it will influence they have positive attitude and interest to choose this kind of leisure consumption. However, if the economic environment is worse, it will influence they have negative attitude and no interest to choose this kind of leisure consumption, due to space travel is one kind of expensive leisure consumption to every one.

Hence, in this space tourism leisure industry, it does not ensure that the rich or high income people must be persuade to choose this kind of expensive space tourism entertainment in whose holiday or retirement time. They can have the common tourism entertainment to go to different countries to travel many times in our earth. Otherwise, space tourism leisure is more expensive to compare common earth tourism leisure , it means that the rich or high income people only spend one time spacecraft catching to fly to space to travel in their life, it is more difficult to every space traveler like to catch spacecraft to fly to space to travel more than one time, due to he/she had attempted to catch spacecraft to fly to space to travel to own space travel experience, he/she will feel enough satisfactory and enjoyment in common. Hence, it is possible that future many rich or high income people only like to spend one time space tourism leisure, then they won't continue to spend this kind of tourism entertainment again in their life.

Thus, space tourism leisure providers need to arrange any special or attractive space tourism leisure to persuade these high income or rich target clients to consume, when the economic environment will change worse. The Europen space agency (ESA), defines this phenomenon between economic environment variable and space tourism client growth or falling number relationship as: " space tourism is an execution of sub-orbital flight by privately finded and/or privately operated vehicles and the technology development driven by space tourism market."

it seems that space vehicle is one attractive travelling desire tool will be one attractive selling point to influence space tourism leisure consumer individual entertainment choice or attitude to be changed to positive leisure consumption attitude to prefer to play this kind of space tourism activities when economic environment changes to worse. Hence, when economic environment is worse, the economic wore changing factor will influence the space travelling planner individual leisure consumption desire, even it will influence the rich or high income young people or rich retirement people target customer both groups.

As (ESA, 2008) indicated space vehicle will be one kind of attractive leisure tool for spce traveler. So, I suggest that space tourism lesiure journey arrangement needs to include that such as : the space travelers can catch space vehicle to move on Moon or Mars plants land to feel what the different feeling is between during they are catching public transportation tool, such as bus or taxi during the are catching these transportation tools on earth land and during they are catching space vehicle tools on Mars or Moon planet's lands. It is so exicting and fun catching space vehicle tool experience on these both Mars or Moon planets' lands to the young and old age space travelling passengers. Because every space vehicle's speed is not very fast and it will move on Moon or Mars planets slowly. So, any aged pace travelling passengers can attempt to play this kind of space facilities leisure after they catched spacecraft to fly to these both Mars or Moon planet to stay. They can spend half hour or one hour, even more than one hour to catch the space vehicle to go to anywhere on Mars or Moon to travel. It is possible that they can find exciting and undiscovered things on these both planets.

So, catching space vehicle to go to anywhere on either these both planets journey, it will one essential part of space travelling journey during the economic environment is changed to worse. It is extra attractive space travelling leisure journey to attract space tourism consumer individual leisure desire when economic environment is worse.

Hence, from this perspective then space tourism could be understood as a section of the tourism industry mainly based on technological development, progression and its activitity being related specifically to sub orbital flights. So, if future space tourism providers expect whether the global economic environment changing will be better or worse which won't influence space tourism leisure consumption desire to be changed. The space tourism leisure providers need to persuade the space tourism planners feel space tourism would have to be treated like an already exciting part of the tourism industry. It means that space tourism leisure is one kind of tourism leisure choice to replace common earth tourism leisure consumption. When travelers feel space tourism is another tourism leisure to replace which can replace common earth tourism leisure. It will avoid the worse economic environment changing factor to reduce the rich or high income young people or rich retirement old people whose space travelling leisure consumption desire.

Consequently , the question in relation to, in what kinds of space tourism journey message do space travel providers promote behind whether space vehicle journey promotion message which is needed when economic environment will change worse. I shall be asked, as understanding the meaning in which space tourism is being marketed, communicated is seen as a factor , which can either positively contribute to future development of the tourism industry or lead into prolonging or seen stopping the space tourism industry from its progression.

(2) Space tourism leisure journey management factor

Secondly, space tourism leisure jounrey management factor, how to arrange every space tourism leisure journey which will be one important factor to influence space tourism planner individual tourism consumption desire.
In general, it can includes these several forms of space tourism leisure activities in every space lesiure trip arrangement. The following classification of space tourism include: Terrestria spce tourism (i.e. NASA visit centre, space movies, online space experience); Atmospheric space tourism (i.e. : MIG 31 flight, zero G. flights) and astro (orbita) tourism (i.e.: trips to the international space station-beyond earth orbit) (Cater 2010, Crouch et al. 2009).
Instead of US domestic space tourism market is potential, next country is Japan. First, the study is made by Collins et. al (1994, 1996) in Japan on 3030 research participants, showed that 80% of respondents under the age of 50 were willing to travel to space and out of them 20% were willing to pay year's salary for the space travel experience. Yet, it could be citicized that the Japan people age group of under 50 could be too broad, in general different generations under one groups. nest besides the willingness to go to space, the Japanese study showed respondents motivations for travelling to space, including any fun and exciting attractive space tourism journey, e.g. interest in space walk, catching space vehicle or driving space vehicle on the either Moon or Mars planets, earth view, zeo gravity experience, livin gin space hotels one night or more, watching movies in space cinemas, swimming in space pools, visiting space gardens, running in space sport centers, catching spacecrafts to view earth or Moon or Mars planets.
Hence, it seems attractive space tourism journey can persuade another country's space travelling planners, such as Japanese attempts to satisfy whose space tourism needs. So, different kinds of attractive space trip journey arrangement will be one important factor to influence young and old age travelling consumption desire. It implies that attractive space tourism journey will be one influential factor to encourage other countries

tourism consumers attempt to another kind of leaving earth tourism leisure. So, any space tourism trip destinations and leisure facilities arrangement must need to satisfy space traveler individual leisure needs and every space trip must be more fun, exciting and comfortable and enjoyable feeling to compare general tourism journey in earth. Due to general earth tourism leisure will be space tourism leisure's competitive or replaced leisure product and service. Hence, space trip destinations and leisure facilities choice will be one important factor to influence space travelling planner's consumption desire.

Every space travelling planner will compare general earth travelling leisure's destinations and leisure facilities arrangement whether the space travelling trip arrangement , leisure facilities arrangement and food arrangement, space vehicle or spacecraf leisure comfortable influence issues which will have more satisfactory enjoyable feeling to compare general earth tourism leisure and their spending expenditure to every space trip whether is value or is not value.

Consequently, economic environment changing factor and space trip and leisure facilities arrangement factor which both will influence any space tourism planner individual consumption desire mainly. So, space tourism businessmen ought concern these two aspects of factors how and when will change to adapt any country's potential space traveler's space tourism changing taste and needs in order to follow the new space tourism changing needs easily.

Hence, from a micro-economic perspective, positive oil price shocks lead to a decline in disposable income. for low income people, it will bring an immediate and negative impact on tourism, mainly due to they feel tourism leisure is regarded as a luxury good, when oil price shocks to rise suddenly . It influences any airline or cruise entertainment service providers‘ costs are influenced to raise. Then, they need to increase air ticket or cruise ticket price. It will bring on negative tourism leisure demands-side the oil price increases low income group, potential tourism leisure consumers. Hence, it seems that oil price may have indirect relationship to influence tourism leisure consumers' needs.

● How the price of oil changes influences global tourism industry growth or recession?

In macro-economic view, sudden mid and long term oil price shock can influence global torusim industry growth or recession. For example, a oil price of US$180 per barrel was considered only a few years ago, now this has a realistic scenario to which all plaers in the T&T sector have to adapt. At such a high level, the price of oil will become even more critical to almost every part of the tourism value chain. Although, weak global demand, caused by global economic recesson, resulted in a steep oil price decline to US$45 per barrel by the fourth quarter of 2008 in the past low oil price occurrence history, this won't change the mid to long -term oil forecast.

In fact, the past oil price occurrence history of the dramatic structural had changed a high price imposed on airlines, travelers, and destination countries, all of which will have to navigate through times of shifting or even declining travel demand. I assume that a high oil price scenario is assumed in the long term in order to highlight the changes , such a senario would mean for consumer behavior and the competitiveness of several destinations.

Low oil price in the 1970 and early 1980 did not bring significant growth of international air travel, but its growth has been strongest between 1980 and 2004, a period with stable and relatively moderate oil prices. Also, the rapid development of the low-cost carrier business model in the 1990s further fueled air travel growth by capturing tourism leisure demand , such as weekend leisure travel to cities using mostly secondary airports in any big area countries, such as UK, US . However, the tourism growth is whole influenced by high oil prices, due to oil price had been continue rising in possible.

Basis of oil is shortage supply product, oil is assumed to be the main energy source for the aviation sector for the nest 30 years. Although, second-generation biofuels seem to be on the horizon, the economics as well as the production scalability and aviation biofuel shortage will be a main challenge to airline industry. So, I assume that oil price will continue rise up, if there have none any aviation biofuel can be reflected to oil to use for air plane energy.

Until 2004, the only factors to have affected air travel growth, negatively were in external shocks , such as 9/11, causes catching air plane crisis or US regional geopolitical conflicts. It brings some travelers feel fear to go to US travel, as well as until recently 2019, human mouth disease can influence air to have disease to anyone from mouth. So, global travelers number had been continue decreasing, because they are fear to get disease by air when many themselves every stranger travelers are sitting on the without windows air planes. Although, mouth human and air disease and US 9/11 air attack both matters may influence oil price falls effect, because air planes flying times will reduce. They won't need frequent to fly, to cause aviation oil energy need reduce. Consequently, oil price will decrease, due to travelers number reduces and air planes flying times are also influenced to reduce. (oil demand decreases cause oil price decrease). Although, air lines ‘ cost will also be influenced reduce, but oil price decrease can not bring travelers number increase , when air ticket price reduce because global many leisure and business trip travelers feel fear to catch air planes frequently when human mouth air disease occured in 2019. So, oil price decreases can not grow up tourism industry growth or rise tourism income.

However, the obvious impact of a high oil price is an increase in the operating costs of airline. Moreover, fuel cost as a percentage of airline operating costs vary significantly based on the length of the flight. The longer the flight, the higher the fuel costs as a percentage of the airline operating cost. So, from an online's perspective, long -hauel flights represent the most criticial challenge to profitable operation because the share of fuel on these flights, compared with other cost items, is largest, because of the unfacorable fuel economics, due to fuel costs even at high-load factors. For example, Thai airways dropped its non-stop Bongkok to US flights in the summer of 2008 for commercial reasons, because fuel reached operating cost levels of 55 percent on this route, a cost burden that could not be passed on to their customers. So, the estimated price elacticity of passengers demand at this Bongkok to US flights route is high, if Thai Airways rises less air ticket price, it will influence many travelers to choose other airlines to catch air plan to fly. Hence, due to Thai Airways can not make decision to rise air ticket price, because it believes that it will lose many travelers, so it only chooses to drop this non-stop Bongkok to US flights to avoid fuel cost rising economic loss.

However, although micro and macro economic theories may also that oil price variable or change, it may influence global tourism income. But, recently, on 2019, human mouth and air diseases, it can influence global individual leisure and business trip travelers feel fear to catch air plans to avoid their bodies get this kind of death sickness when they sit in the no fresh air supplying air planes. They feel that they reduce leisure travelling flying times or business trip flying times with strange travelers to sit in crowd air planes together. Then, they must many avoid human moth and air disease to avoid death crisis. Hence, in this global human mouth and air diseases threat environment occurrence, even oil price sudden reduces to low price, it brings airline's cost reduces and air ticke price reduces. However, when air ticket price reduce to be very cheaper, it can not still attract global many leisure or business trip travelers to buy air tickets to fly frequently. Why does air ticket reduction, it can not attract many leisure or businee trip travelers to buy air ticket to fly ? The main reason is because human mouth and air disease influences global many travelers feel fear to catch air planes frequently. In psychological view, this kind of human mouth and air sickness will bring long time negative influence to global traveles do not want to catch air planes for business trips or travelling leisure frequently. So, it implies that oil price changing to influence air ticket price reduction factor ought not main factor to influence tourism income. It may include traveler individual negative emotion psychological factor, such as human mouth and air disease or 2019 9/11 attack both cases, they can influence global travelers feel fear to catch air planes to fly to avoid death threat. So, oil changing price ought not be only one absolute main factor to influence global tourism income significantly.

On conclusion, in economic view, it seems that oil chang price may have indirect or direct relationship to influence tourism income, instead of some unpredicted external environment factors influence, such as US 9/11 attack crisis and human mouth and air disease factors, they may be main factors to influence travellers number to reduce in non-economic external unpredicted environment view. But, in fact, COVID 19 disease may be the main factor to influence global oil need reduces and price reduces .

● How to develop new economic tourism industry after COVID 19 disease disappears ?

How to develop tourism industry in new economic environment? Any examination of the new economic development of travel and tourism requires definitions of the subject and its components, which are suitable for economic analysis. However, in new economic development to tourism industry, it is also important to look at tourism conceptually, in order to set the scene for a deeper understanding of the future new tourism industry development.

Tourism is neither a phenomenon nor a simple set if industries, however, in new or old economic development environment. It is a human activity which encompasses human behavior, use of resources, and interaction with other people, economies and leisure enjoyment environment. It is also involved physical movement of tourists to locales other than their normal living places.

In future new economic environment, traditional travel needs to include these element in order to satisfy traveler enjoyment and leisure feeling: They may include: Tourist needs and motivations, tourism selection and behavior and constraints , travel away from home , market interactions between tourists and those supplying products to satisfy tourist needs and impacts on tourists , hosts, economies and environments.

In new economic environment, the tourism products may include: carriers, in any forms of transport for tourist travel accommodation, man-made attractions, which could also include the managed areas of natural attractions, private sector and public sector support services, middlemen, such as tour wholesalers and travel agents.

The tourism resources may also include: Natural resources, lands , minerals, water and biological; labor resources, human work, and enterprise; capital resources, manmade enhancement and other resources. The travel and tourism resources problems may include: As there is frequently a mismatch between producer and consumer perception of what constitutes the tourism product , there may be conflict in ideas of which resources are properly involved as well as many of the resources likely to be in demand for tourism are public goods , or even free resources.

In new economic development to tourism industry view, we need to consider that tourism and travel has the reputation of being a relatively clean and pleasant industry in which to work or invest in order to attract a greater number of resource suppliers than as less well-perceived industry, which therefore keeps rewards prices down by competition, how to attract those retiring from or travel business for example, if their finances are already sound, income from travel is not expected to be optimal , travel and tourism is frequently highly seasonal , offering rewards that are competitive with other industries only some of the time, destination products are often in locations which are of little use to other industries, so that competition for resource use if minimal and hence rewards are low.

In general, tourist purpose may include: recreational purpose : holiday, health and sport and religion as well as business purpose: company business , e.g. conventions and sales trips. So, in new economic tourism development aim, tourism industry need consider hoe to achieve incentive trips to let these both tourists to feel. For example, the overall type of tourism required, destination arrangement, travel mode, accommodation and attraction visiting and purchasing method or distribution channel. The purchasing method choices may include: whether to buy an inclusive package or separate service, whether to buy direct from suppliers, such as airlines or hotels or use an agent , which tour wholesaler or operate or agent to use.

I predict the tourism development in new economic view, it may have these characteristics: Few enterprises in travel and tourism are large, highly cashed-up and have a large asset base, enterprises within travel and tourism that are not in a financial position to diversify, and those do well success to the above –average growth obtainable in travel and tourism compared with many other industries, they would therefore tend to expand within the sector. The result of individual enterprise growth and integration within travel and tourism is an increase in the concentration of that industry. The degree to which output is produced of fewer and fewer enterprises. This can be only be accounted for realistically with the context of an individual economy, Levels of concentration in any part of travel and tourism in the future are likely to depend on two opposing factors: The constant demand by many tourist market segments for new experiences and products, which encourages the development and survival of more and diverse enterprises, and therefore leads to the reduction of concentration as well as technology, which in travel and tourism frequently calls for large capital outlays and requires mass markets for efficient use, promotes integrations and large scale enterprise, especially in air travel and non-personal services (marketing and information communication, travel insurance , tourism payment methods). IN these areas, concentration will undoubtedly increase in future new economic development environment.

● How new economic development in oil industry after COIV 19 disease

The future global economic growth, it will influence personal incomes and GDP rise. They would carry different weight in different countries at different times. Starting from low levels of incomer and economic development. Household consumption will change from being dominated by basic heat to rapidly rising energy use for higher levels of comfort in space heating and cooling (and large dwellings), and greater use of electrical appliances, finally to a degree of saturation influenced by the income distribution patterns of the country concerned. Income distribution typically changes very slowly, so that the technical market for heart will never be saturated because there will always be a proportion of poor people living in small spaces less comfortably than the average. Industrial energy consumption will be influenced by technical efficiency within each sector, and by changes in the structures of the economy, e.g. changing proportions of agriculture, heavy and light industry, and services. One may eventually see evidence of diminishing marginal returns to additional energy inputs compared to other inputs. Energy consumption in the energy transformation sector may be influenced by income, which drives the demand for electricity to influenced by income, which drives the demand for electricity to grow faster than the demand for heat, but is also subject to the chosen technology of transformation, which is influenced by the cost and availability of primary energy inputs (fuels) in new economic development environment.

IN new economic development environment, it will influences that fuels do not compete in all sectors; for example, the transport sector is dominated by oil. Nuclear and hydroelectric power (and most renewables) reach the user through electricity; electricity itself competes with the direct burning of fossil fuels. Electricity provides the means by which other fuels can compete with oil and gas in sectors, such as space heating and process heat. It also is the only means of powering applications such as motors, computers and lighting: these subsectors are difficult to analyze. However, there is strong evidence that higher incomes do not weaken the demand for electricity so much as the demand for energy in total (in contrast to the effect on the demand for non-electric energy forms).

Econometricians look at the historical record of change in fuel prices and quantities to distinguish several factors between the new economic development and old economic development to oil industry in the future. An income effect. Increasing (reducing) fuel prices reduces (increases) the purchasing power of consumers' income: higher incomes caused by lower prices will increase energy consumption; the consumers' allocation of the increased income to energy purchases may reduce as income rises. Thus income may be heading in a different direction from fuel prices that the effect of fuel price changes when incomes are rising means simply that rising incomes have increased demand. Reducing the cost of using energy through win-win efficiency measures causes a similar problem . On the consequence, in future new economic development environment, it may influence in both cases demand will be less than if the future oil price or efficiency has not changed. The other effect is that an efficiency or substitution effect. An increase in fuel prices may cause consumers to spend more on new equipment, building materials and management operations, which will reduce the amount of fuel required to give the same energy result to the user. The extent of the efficiency effect depends on what happens to the price of the new equipment or building: if those price s rise in line with the fuel price, changes in the balances between fuel and capital or management will not occur. A new user technology , such as the development of the combined cycle gas turbine generator may increase efficiency and thus greatly reduce the quantity of primary fuel needed to produce the required output in this case electricity. If electricity prices had remained sticky, and the electricity and gas markets were not competitive, some of this advantages could have accrued to the gas suppliers in the form of an increase in price, because th4 unit of gas produces more output of electricity, it would have a higher value. In reality, the development of new economic competitive environment in both gas and electricity has tended to ensure that the benefits of such technical advanced accrue to the consumer through lower final prices. The same many apply in the case of improved efficiency in future non-manual driving auto vehicle development: the consumer's cost of motoring is reduced in new economic non-manual driven auto vehicle (Artificial intelligent vehicle) can replace manual driven vehicle , even electricity battery can replace oil energy to be used in vehicles. So, oil price may be influenced to reduce in future new economic development environment.

Airport service life cycle stage improvement strategy can improve future tourism industry to grow up after COVID 19 disease disappears ?

Any organizations will have life cycle stage from birth, growth , mature to decline. In airport service organizations have theis life cycle stages in service aspect. Airports organizatins aim to provide safe, comfortable , even shopping environment to let passengers to stay and to wait to transfer another air planes to visit another destination or arrive the country's airport to check out or check in to enter the airport to leave. If airports have life cycle stages, what the characteristics to every stage? How to improve airport service in order to reach mature life cycle stage rapidly? How to implement airport service strategy in order to reach mature life cycle stage to the aorport organization rapidly?I shall explain as below:

Any airports need to be planned in order to raise excellent service to let passengers to let any travelers choose to travel the country whether the country can provide excellent service and facilities. It will bring indirect emotion impact to influence the travelers chooce to revisit the country to travel again. However, soft or hard element or) staff service performance or airport facility), they will influence whether the different countries travelers to choose to travel to re-visit the country again. So, learning how to keep the mature or airport service life cycle stage to stay long time, it will be one important factor to influence any airport business in success.

In the birth life style stage to airport, airport organizations must maintain the capability to provide expert advice to airport owners an matters including operational safety, during construction, environmental compatibility, and airport development standards. No other private or public organization can be expected maintain this level of proficiency. These value-added services enhance public trust when assuring consistant application of standards for the nation's airport system. So, it seems that when the new airport is built if it hopes its passenger customers can consider themselves emotion need. So, it ought concentrate on nowadays airplane landing cunways or airport transfer free service transport etc. facilities can let them to feel safe when they were walking in any airport places. If they feel anywhere are dangerous when they are walking or staying in the ne sirport, then new airport non safe or dangerous factor may influence travelers to choose the country to travel again.

Any new airports will need have good new national airport plan in order to it might operate in the near future with respect to safety areas. The plan elements may include as below:

Achieving zero accidents aim, establish standard safety areas at all commercial service airports , achieving the most minimum 85% of all passenger flights operate on runways with safe feeling, increase measure to 100% of all passenger flight operating on runways with standard safety areas after three months. Within 5 years, 95% of all passenger flights begin and end on runways with standard safety areas.

On benefits aspect, aims to mobilize work force to improve safety area performance describes realistic investment benefits. So, in any new airports birth life cycle stage, they must need to consider safety and expenditure for repair aspect in order to keep its service performance to avoid passengers have dissatisfactory feeling when they are staying in their new airports.

When the country has many travelers travel to the country , then the country's new airport passengers number must increase. It is its the new airport growth life cycle stage. These are critical success factors influence the airport, whether it can improve service performance in order to excite different countries travelers visiting the country's airport desire or grow up the visitors number successfully. The critical success factors may include: Having necessary support from internal and externa stakeholders to implement and willing to share information and identify anywhere the total airport facilities of repair needs that are both reliable and feasible projections to let passengers to feel more safe feeling when they are staying in the airport, understand its future service vision and mission, set strategic direction and goals to process/product specific objectives and decision-making across and doen the organization, define, model and prioritize planning prcesses critical for mission performance, practice hand-on sernior management ownership of planning process and allow field, personnel flexiblity in performing jobs, adjust organizational structures , an essessment program to evaluate planning process and product management , e.g. national airport system performance, create organizational understanding of the value management to customer and stakeholder current and future expectations developing human resources management strategies to support new process that solves needs planners and engineers, building information resources strategies change, especially for entering data at the source and maintains data integrity and timeliness.,establish central support group to support reengineering efforts, outreach and training efforts across the organization, phase in short-and long-term results that achieve set goals and objectives over the next two years.

Thus, when one new airport begins to feel passengers number is increasing. It ought experience the growth life cycle stage to the new airport , if it hopes that it can reach mature life cycle stage rapidly as well as keeps its mature life cycle stage to stay in this stage long time or reachs the airport service performance to the most satisfactory level in this mature life cycle stage. It must need to attempt to plan these strategies to implement in order to avoid decline life cycle stage occurs in short time. So, it explains why some new airport can experience the development to mature life cycle stage from grow life cycle stage in short time,even when it reachs mature life cycle stage. It can keep to stay in this stage long time. The reason is that it had prepared effective strategies to achieve how to improve its airport service performance aim in order to satisfy passenger needs. When they are staying in the country's airport any time. Hence, every year revising service performance is needed to any airports.

Any airports must have development processes. The question is that whether the airport needs how long time to reach growth or mature life cycle stage from birth stage or decline life cycle stage will be delayed how long to occur. The development processes may mean that the airport development life cycle stages changes that had toard a particular result or even as a series of continuous actions or operations coducting to an end (Merriam-Webster, 2013).

reference

Merriam-webster (2013). On line dictionary. Available at:
https://www.merriam-webster. com/(last accessed July , 8 2013).

Hence, any airport organizations with experience development pricess. When the new airport is built, it must be in the birth life cycle stage. Its passengers number can not increase rapidly. It needs time to grow their number. But, when the new airport operates a period, many different countries begin feel this new airport is existence in the country. They will attempt to catch airplance to visit this country airport to catch airplane to visit tis country airport to travel. If they feel this country airport service performance can satisfy their short time staying feeling or its passengers or airports visitors number may increase rapidly. It meand that this airport is experiencing growth life cycle stage. So, if the airport can attract many visitors in short time. It will reduce time to growth life cycle stage from birth life cycke stage.

So , service performance may be one important factor to inflow the airport grows. When the airport develops to the period, passengers number can not increase rapidly, it may be the airport's mature life cycle stage. Due to it's passengers number can not grow rapidly, its passengers number also may reduce. When its passengers number has significant decrease, if its reduction number is increasing more. It implies that the airport is experiencing decline life cycle stage. All any country's airport may experience whole life cycle stages. If the country's airport can not implement successful strategies, it may experience birht life cycle stage in long time because it can not grow its passengers number significantly. So, any airports need to learn how to help them to change growth life cycle stage, even mature life cycle stage can stay in long time easily. If they hope to attract many different countries passengers to visit their airports or travel themselves countries or enjoy to stay short time in themselves airports in order to grow themselves airline industry development.

- How can processes improvement management strategy influence airport service performance?

Overall processes in an airport may involve passengers, luggage, cargo, aircraft movements, ground handling, and crews . All of these operations can be systematised into processes at airport terminal. Three main types of processes can be established departing , arrival and transfer . Departure consists in catching a flight to a final or intermediate destination, arrival consists in landing and leaving the airport, and transfer consists in landing at the airport only to catch another flight to a final or an intermediate destination. Airports also deal with cargo. It involves in the movement of cargo by air, cargo fies from the shopper to the consignee through one or more airlines. However, when the airport can let them freight forwarder, being familiar with the necessary procedures how permits the airline to concentrate on the provision of air transport and to avoid time consuming details of the facilitation and landside distribution system. It will raise efficiency and improve service performance. The services product by the ground handling are crucial to the success and efficiency of the airport operations.

These services are usually provided by specialised companies. Briefly, it includes the luggage treatment, passengers carrying from plan to terminal when needed and aircraft assistance. Also, focusing on crew, there are two majoe processes, one for departures and the other for arrivals. The crew members also have to pass the security and passport controls. However, they have special channels for this. Once they reach the aircraft, the similarities with the passengers' procedure stop. Hence, they have to perform a set of activities , such as check the aircraft load sheets and help passengers to name a few. Also airport terminal operations processes for passengers and luggage, typically for departures , passengers do the check on the airline area, pass security controls, proceed to the general lounge and lastly to the gate holding area. arriving passengers are able to immediately go from the luggage claim area, but the non-passengers have to pass the passport control at first. After this passengers have to decide if they need to declare goods or not as the paths are different . Hence, if the airport can reduce all of this service processes are less complex as immigration check in-out service, liggage claim can be efficient to carry when passengers need to find themselves luggage. Then, it will reduce waste time and let they satisfy airport service absolutely. So, reducing service process time amy also help the airport to increase customers number significantly. When airport role is the middleman between airlines , cargo transport service providers and passengers, e.g. short time transport cargo service and reducing passengers check in or check out service time. then, it will let them to feel more satisfactory service to the airport.

Hence, airport capacity is as a multifactor function leaves open the exact relationship between the factors but stresses that all factors are relevant to assess airport capacity . So , understanding airport capacity and what drives the capacity usage at airports may provide an insight in the set of instructments available to optimise the use of capacity. All of these factors may influence any capacity of an airport, they may include as below:

For example, technical constraints, e.g. ATM per hour service in a runway in a combined arrival and departure fashion, when many passengers are staying at the airport, they can withdraw money from ATM easily. So, ATM number facilities service supply number and location choice to the airport factors will infuence passengers ‘ satisfactory level, another factor is environmental constraints, it can directly offer the wellbeing of the communities surrounding the negative emotion to passengers and communities surrounding the airprt. For this factor, the change in technology and/or operational procedures can provide more capacity in the system.

Airline business models factor, it can affect the capacity spoke model when other under a point-point one ,these models directly affect the peak hour operational capacity, particularly in big international hubs. Airlines often compete with high frequencies between destinations, thus increasing the number of movements. In addition, conncectivity also has downsides for this model: the delays in one airport might be exported and sometimes in another, due to the connectivity influencing the real capacity. This factor has been setting economic incentives or pricing models. Furthermore, expanding information systems, from one airport to multiple airports gate-to-gate concept, and the use of larger airport to redcuce frequencies.

Hence, above these factors may influence whether the airport needs how long time to reach maturiry life cycle stage when it is staying the growth life cycle stage. It depends on how its strategies implementation and how environment influence its implementation , if it hopes to achieve to reach the maturity life cycle stage in success in short time.

Finally, I shall explain life cycle cst analysis to any country pavement strategy will bring what significant influential benefits to any airports continue to develop in order to avoid to reach decline life cycle stage time in short time easily , when they are staying in the mature life cycle stage. In the construction or rehabilitation investments of highway’s pavements, it is already common to perform a life-cycle analysis or life cycle cost analysis for different alternatives to airport pavements. Becauae when any airport pavements are using for a long time, every day has many airplanes need to fly to land on the pavement. It can bring significant repace influence when the airport has many airplanes are needed to land on the pavements every day in the maturity life cycle stages.

Hence, how to evaluate the repair cost expenditure budget in order to satisfy every day air planes land on the airport pavement need. In the calculations are different cost factors (including direct and indirect cost)to any airport itself pavement. Direct costs are related to the critical construction cost landing on pavement activities and are calculated with information from the airport agency and constructors that work for them. The indirect costs are related with the loss of daily revenue of the airport during work activities, such as landing on the airport pavement.

Runways are the most critical pavements area of airport , so it is critical to ensure the quality of these pavement to let airplanes to land on the airport safety, e.g. they need to be constructed with sufficient strength to carry the moving airport and have a high resistance to skidding and aquaplaining. It is most of the time accomplished with reconstructions or deep rehabilitation. Hence, predicting how much will spend on airport pavement facilities expenditure must need in every day.

However, the life cycle assessment (LCA) is a mult step procedure for calculating the life time environmental impact of a product or service is needed to any airport organizations, when they reachs maturity life cycelt stage . The complex process includes goal and cope definition in inventory analysis impact assessment. The process is vaturally iteractive as quality and completeness of information is constantly being testes. When the definition of the aim and scope of the study is done the next step is the development of an inventory, in which all significant environmental burdens during the lifetime of the product,, such as airport pavements or process , such as airplanes landing on the pavement or airplanes leaving from the pavement in the airport.

(Araujo, Oliveria & Silve) 2014 explained that life cycle snslysis of pavements are focused on the activities of extraction, production, transportation application of materials, concisely the construction of the road. Because its difficult to obtain other relevant data knowing that the use phase of the pavement is predominant with repect to energy consumption and also to gas emissions related to the atmosphere. One of the main factors for the use phase is the rolling resistance, this depends on the surface and structural characteristics of the different pavements.

Hence, , if the airport can have good repairment or renew skills to help its pavement to improve. Then, it may bring long time benefit, such as reducing airplanes energy consumption and also to avoid gas emissions or reduce gas emissions accident occurrene, even air plane landing on pavement accident occurrence chance can reduce to the zero. so, defining the expected pavement performance time improvement strategy can influence whether the airport pavement can satisfy all airplane users how long time landing on or leaving on the airport pavement. Also it is the major factor to influence airport main function success for any airplanes arriving to the country's airport pavement or leaving from the country's airport pavement. Hence, calculating any airport pavement life cycle costs factor. It is necessary to analysis and interpret carefully the results to identfy the most economic pavement strategy in any airport's whole life cycle development stages.

reference

Araujo, J.P.C. Oliveria, J.R.M. & Silva H.M.R.D. (2011) . the importance of the use phase on the LCA of environmentally friendly solutions for asphalt road pavements. transportation research part D: trasport and environment, 32(0), 97-110. Retrieved in March 2015 from://
dx. doi.org/10.1016/j.trd.2014.07.006.

How COVID 19 disease influences cruise leisure need

In fact, the cruise and air tourism leisure activiites are very similar, travellers will be influenced to bring negative emotion when they need to travel on the cruise or catch air planes to go to another country o travel by COVID 19 disease influence. The COVID-19 pandemic has a huge impact on the tourism industry due to the resulting travel restrictions as well as slump in demand among travelers. The tourism industry has been massively affected by the spread of coronavirus, as many countries have introduced travel restrictions in an attempt to contain its spread. The United Nations World Tourism Organization estimated that global international tourist arrivals might decrease by 58% to 78% in 2020, leading to a potential loss of US$0.9–1.2 trillion in international tourism receipts. In many of the world's cities, planned travel went down by 80–90%. Conflicting and unilateral travel restrictions occurred regionally and many tourist attractions around the world, such as museums, amusement parks, and sports venues closed. UNWTO reported a 65% drop in international tourist arrivals in the first six months of 2020. Air passenger travel showed a similar decline. So, it seems that COVID 19 disease may influence cruise passengers number decrease.

How COVID 19 disease influences cruise pasengers their tourism leisure on sea to Singapre and Australia cruise leisure passengers number and insurance medical expenses to cruise passenger are raised ?

I shall indicate Caribban ship in Singapore case example as below:

A Royal Caribbean ship in Singapore that had been forced to turn around after reporting a positive case of COVID-19, has confirmed the passenger did not actually have the virus. Singaporean officials confirmed to CNN this week that the 83-year-old man who tested positive reported a false positive test.

Following protocol after the initial news of his testing positive earlier this week, fellow passengers in close contact with him were placed under quarantine and the crew began a contact tracing process. The quarantined passengers will be compensated for the days of travel they missed, the cruise line told CNN. "We have rescinded the Quarantine Orders of his close contacts, who had earlier been placed on quarantine as a precautionary measure while investigations were ongoing," Royal Caribbean said in a statement.

This was the ship's third sailing since it resumed "ocean getaway voyages" with no port calls. The ship, which was operating at 50% capacity, had left Singapore on Dec. 7 and was in its second day of sailing when the supposed case was discovered, Cruise Critic reported.

Passengers and crew who are not considered close contacts with the thought to be infected guest (1,679 passengers and 1,148 crew) remained on the ship and were allowed to disembark and were not forced to isolate. In order to board the ship, passengers were required to test negative for COVID-19 within three days of the start of the trip and wear a contact tracing-enabled wristband while on board. Only Singapore residents were allowed to board.

The cruise line relaunched sailings in Singapore, but has cancelled most of its planned itineraries elsewhere through Feb. 28. And while Royal Caribbean is looking for volunteers to test new health protocols in the U.S. (part of the Centers for Disease Control and Prevention's 'Conditional Sail' Order), it was not immediately clear when those would take place.

Royal Caribbean isn't alone in trying to resume sailings only for those efforts to be stymied by an outbreak of the virus on board. SeaDream Yacht Club restarted sailings in the Caribbean last month, but was forced to turn around when several passengers and crew tested positive for coronavirus. Thus, it seems that COVID 19 disease may influencce Singapore cruise lesiure destination passengers number decreases.

As a result of the pandemic, many countries and regions have imposed quarantines, entry bans, or other restrictions for citizens of or recent travellers to the most affected areas. Other countries and regions have imposed global restrictions that apply to all foreign countries and territories, or prevent their own citizens from travelling overseas.Together with a decreased willingness to travel, the restrictions have had a negative economic impact on the travel sector in those regions. A possible long-term impact has been a decline of business travel and international conferencing, and the rise of their virtual, online equivalents.Concerns have been raised over the effectiveness of travel restrictions to contain the spread of COVID-19.

For how COVID 19 disease influences Australia cruise industry example, tourism bodies have suggested that the total economic cost to the sector, as of 11 February 2020, would be A$4.5 billion. Casino earnings are expected to fall. At least two localities in Australia, Cairns and the Gold Coast, have reported already lost earnings of more that $600 million.The Australian Tourism Industry Council (ATIC) called on the Government of Australia for financial support especially in light of the large number of small businesses affected. In March, national travel agency Flight Centre has indefinitely closed 100 stores throughout Australia, due to significantly lower demand for travel.It also suffered a 75% decline in share price, and announced that 6,000 staff would be made redundant or placed on unpaid leave globally.

On the 781-foot vessel's Promenade deck, an art gallery abuts a big-screen movie theater. The Lido deck has a fitness center and full-service spa.

That cornucopia of amenities has greeted guests on largely smooth sailings over the past 20 years. But by late March, the vessel had been transformed into an isolation ward, and by the time the ship finally docked in Florida in early April, four passengers had died, two of whom had been diagnosed with Covid-19.

The cruise industry, which the Cruise Lines International Association says was worth $150 billion worldwide in 2018, is now assessing the damage. Even as the coronavirus continues to spread, though, some key industry players are already seeing signs of growth in the coming years. A cruise industry resurgence would send thousands back to work and send travelers back to sunny ports across the globe. While some cruisers are eager to book, other tentative travelers have concerns about their health, medical emergencies and their money.

Can COVI19 disease cause the cruise industry service staffs lose jobs?

In a quarterly report released on April 3, Carnival Corporation, the world's largest travel leisure company, predicted that the coronavirus impact could be grave.

"We have never previously experienced a complete cessation of our cruising operations," the report reads, noting the high costs of repatriating passengers, assisting quarantined crew and the possibility of lawsuits related to the corporation's handling of the pandemic. Wedbush analyst James Hardiman recently estimated Carnival was burning $500 million in cash reserves each month.

But Carnival stock -- which by March 18 had dropped over 82% from a high in mid-January -- got a boost when Saudi Arabia officials announced on April 6 that the country's sovereign wealth fund had acquired an 8% stake in the company.

How cruise travelers can protect themselves ?

Given the ongoing risk of coronavirus, some cruisers are looking to travel insurance as a way to ensure their medical treatment would be covered if they contract the illness. While coverage varies between companies and policies, Scott Adamski, head of US field sales for AIG Travel, wrote in an emailed statement that many standard plans cover onboard treatment from the ship's doctor, treatment at port or transport to another medical facility. Medical evacuation, which can be very expensive when paid out of pocket, is also covered by some plans. That evacuation could range from commercial flights with a medical-provider escort to an air ambulance; Adamski stressed the importance of learning the details of an individual plan before making a purchase. In the wake of the coronavirus crisis, thousands of cruisers have looked to companies for refunds or credits. Most cruise lines have offered flexible policies around cancellation and rebooking amid the pandemic.

But as travel industry struggles to cope with the disruption, some are wondering what will happen if future bookings are canceled as well. Travel insurance can help, but as with health issues, the details of individual plans vary widely.

Travel insurance would likely not cover travelers if the cruise company cancels the cruise, according to Adamski. Travelers, he notes, should contact the cruise company for a refund or voucher. (Another option Adamski suggests is to contact your credit card company, which may have some provisions for cancellations of trips you booked on the card.)

For example, if a traveler decides to cancel a cruise because of their own concerns about coronavirus, Adamski believes that a refund via travel insurance is unlikely. Covered reasons for cancellation are listed in individual policies, and generally include things such as medical emergencies and weather events. Hence, cruise lesiure companies need to help cruise passengers to buy health and medical insurance to avoid their compensation loss , due to COVD19 disease can attack any one passenger when he/she goes on the cruise to travel in the cruise travelling days, e.g. one week, one month, even, three months or more times. So, when any one cruise passenger spends long time to stay on the cruise, he/she will get the COVID 19 disease easily when he/she needs to contact to any one cruise staff, e.g. cleaner, restaurant waiter, crew, even cruise passenger. Hence, COVID 19 disease may also influence many cruise passengers feel fear to choose cruise to travel, even they won't decide to stay long time on the cruise. Consequently, they may be influenced by COVID 19 disease either shortening cruise time to week, short cruise journey or canceling any cruise journeys easily.

On conclusion, air and cruise travellers will be influenced to reduce travelling leisure activities, even air ticket and cruise ticket prices are decreasing by COVID 19 disease. Also, it implies that COVD 19 disease may be the most influential factor to compare economic recession, pollution, inflation, unemployment rate rising etc. factors to reduce future travellers number in global.

Illness how influences Economic Recsssion

COVID 19 disease how influences consumer individual
visiting shopping behavior

As the virus swept the globe, brands changed how they interacted with customers due to social distancing and stay-at-home orders. Consumer buying patterns also shifted with fluctuations in the stock market, skyrocketing unemployment and supply chain issues. As many people lost their jobs and those still earning a paycheck worried about future layoffs, impulse purchasing became infrequent. Messages that resonated with consumers a few weeks prior suddenly fell flat and even seemed insensitive.

In the early weeks of the pandemic response, many brands implemented a crisis marketing strategy, pivoting messaging and offers as quickly as possible. Hotels.com shifted ads with its mascot, Captain Obvious, from partying with friends to eating popcorn alone with a bottle of hand sanitizer. Panera launched Panera Grocery, enabling customers to buy high-demand grocery items it already stocks in its restaurants—such as bread, produce and milk—along with soups and sandwiches. In an effort to help parents with kids at home full time, Time for Kids magazine gave anyone access to its 2020 digital editions for free, and Amazon Prime provided kids with free video content.

COVID 19 disease can influence consumers need to attempt to adapt to new virtual consumption behaviors

As stay-at-home and social distancing orders took hold in the spring, customers relied even more heavily on digital and mobile platforms as their smartphones became a lifeline to the outside world. New virtual behaviors emerged and expanded as consumers completed their daily tasks digitally, such as curbside pickup, telehealth appointments, online workouts and contact-free delivery. And as many people worked from home, went to school online, and connected with family and friends virtually, video chat use exploded. The video chat platform Zoom saw a staggering 418% growth in adoption rate in two just months. In response to these new behaviors, brands proactively showed customers how they fit into new routines and expectations. Pizza Hut rolled out tamper-proof seals, making it apparent if anyone has opened a pizza box before it gets to the intended destination. Beauty brand MAC created a tool to let customers virtually try on lipstick and eye shadow since they could no longer sample colors at a makeup counter or MAC store.

How coronavirus impacts consumer behavior

Consumer needs are changing as a result of the pandemic. The way people interact with brands—and how they view themselves as consumers—is fundamentally different than it was pre-quarantine. Spicer has seen three major shifts in consumer buying habits:

Home: People are spending more time in their homes, which has both practical and emotional effects. A conversation Spicer had with Samsung centered on how people are rethinking the role that products such as home appliances now play. Not only do appliances need to work, but people have other considerations as well, such as: Is my washing machine quiet enough to have a Zoom call in the next room? Does the vacuum clean deep enough to remove germs? Where are appliance materials sourced from?

By quickly adding online lessons to its product offerings, Guitar Center took advantage of the national mindset of setting goals for self-improvement projects during stay-at-home orders. Through social media and email, the retailer stayed in contact while encouraging people to make music at home. And for those not quite yet ready to learn new chords, Guitar Center shared musical videos of popular, professional guitar players for inspiration.

Consumer shopping habits and behavior shift constantly, but in pre-COVID times, brands could normally pivot on smaller scales to make a difference—like offering gluten-free options or making content available on streaming platforms. Coming out of the pandemic, people are thinking about their role as consumers differently, which will force brands to make larger fundamental changes to anticipate new consumer needs.

Physically, people are now on devices and networks that weren't previously commingled—such as work computers on home IP addresses. Additionally, more individuals in the house are on those Wi-Fi networks across devices, making unique identification complicated. More existentially, people are craving relationships and connection. They're likely not expecting brands to fill that need, but any brand that does will be rewarded for its efforts.

"COVID-19 is going to affect the platforms you use, the content you create, the offers you design and campaigns to support those offers," Solis says. "Essentially, you have the opportunity to start from scratch and build those touchpoints, hopefully investing heavily in artificial intelligence and machine learning across the journey."

Because COVID-19 impacts consumers differently across states and geographic areas, brand marketers should carefully think through how a range of consumers will react. How will your campaign play in big cities like Atlanta or New York and in smaller towns in rural areas? And how do you shift the messaging based on location?

Concern over health and safety, especially personal contact and large groups, will likely remain with us for months and possibly years. While some pre-COVID-19 behaviors will return at some point, many of the changes that occurred during the pandemic are likely to become permanent, especially new habits like video chats with family, telehealth visits with doctors and virtual workouts at home.

Brands should look to build their infrastructure and future products to support this likely permanent shift to using virtual platforms and options when possible. Even without mandatory social distancing guidelines, many consumers will continue to favor online activities due to the convenience factor.

The cornerstone of marketing has always been creating connections with customers. The pandemic created a new world where relationships with both people and brands became more important than ever. By closely monitoring ever-shifting customer sentiment and priorities, and leveraging tools to ramp up personalization, businesses can leave the crisis with new long-term customers.

COVID 19 disease may bring below negative visiting shopping emotion influence to global consumers

New global consumer research shows how consumers are radically changing their lives in response to the pandemic. Many consumers are facing new personal situations, with changes in income and leisure time, which are influencing attitudes and behaviors. Consumers are shopping with greater awareness of the environment, health and cost, favoring locally-sourced products and neighborhood stores. The huge rise in digital commerce, especially among new or low-frequency consumers, is likely to continue post-pandemic.

Retail consumer behavior is changing at unprecedented speed

The COVID-19 global pandemic is having a profound impact on consumers' lives. As stay-at-home orders and country-wide lockdowns start to be eased, consumer behavior continues to be driven by new personal circumstances, such as changes in discretionary income and spare time, and reconsidered values and priorities.

Retail consumers adapt to new personal circumstances

Changes to disposable income and available leisure time are influencing consumers' attitudes, behaviors and purchasing habits. For example, 33%

of consumers are finding themselves 'financially-squeezed', with less disposable income compared to before the crisis, and are shopping more cost consciously, whereas 26% (the 'Resource-Rich') have increased both their disposable income and free time, and are enjoying new leisure pursuits.

In markets where the pandemic is stabilizing, economic concerns remain high, denting consumer confidence. And although fears about health are gradually subsiding, consumers remain uncomfortable about visiting public places, although they are relatively more comfortable with familiar places such as grocery and pharmacy stores.69% of consumers in stabilizing markets and 80% in advancing markets are fearful for the health of others

Retail consumers adopt conscious and mindful purchasing habits

Consumers are more mindful than ever about what they are buying—and it's a mindset that's likely to continue. The majority (75%) are limiting food waste, and 67% are shopping more health-consciously. In both cases, 90% of these consumer groups are likely to continue with these habits.

Demand for local goods is growing, as consumers seek out products they feel they can trust, and efficiency is also on consumers' minds, as they are doing fewer and larger shopping trips. Overall, there are 10 consumer trends impacting goods purchased. 64% of consumers agree that governments and businesses will increase their focus on the environment.

Retail consumers embrace digital commerce and omnichannel

With lock-downs in place and many stores shuttered, ecommerce has surged. Adoption has accelerated from previously uninitiated users, especially in under-penetrated categories such as grocery. Consumers have also increased their use of omnichannel services like contactless payment, social commerce, virtual consultations and curbside pickup. It's new behavior that they plan to continue.

Retail consumers find creative ways to fill their time at home

With more time spent at home, consumers are engaging in new or renewed activities during their spare time. More than half (62%) are trying new recipes, 51% are spending time on home improvements, and 48% are embarking on new skills or online education. In each case, the vast majority expect to continue with these activities.

Families are welcoming the opportunity to spend more time together, and new ways of socializing are gaining in popularity as people connect virtually. With the switch in many cases to working from home, employees have embraced their new environments and many expect to continue or increase their time spent home working in the future.

Consequently, the retail industry has experienced major disruptions in the past, but consumer preferences and shopping patterns have never shifted so quickly. As well as changing how they shop, the reasons why consumers shop has also changed forever. Retailers need to draw on data-driven insights to renew their relationship with consumers.

Responsibility to employees and consumers has taken on a new significance. When it comes to restarting the economy, the near-ubiquitous lack of consumer confidence will pose an enormous challenge. Retailers need to build trust with consumers, such as implementing visible safety and hygiene measures for staff and customers in stores.

COVID 19 disease how brings online shopping
behavior chance

The huge rise in digital commerce, especially among new or low-frequency consumers, is likely to continue post-pandemic.Nowadays,
COVID 19 disease had influence global visiting shop consumers choose to buy any products from online. I shall indicate US online shopping development trend example as below:

Months into the coronavirus disease 2019 (COVID-19) pandemic, Americans' online shopping habits are continuing to shift. We documented changes in online shopping habits at the beginning of the pandemic, comparing patterns from January and February (before the pandemic) with patterns from mid-March and April (when lockdowns and other restrictions were beginning).

We now present findings from an August 2020 RAND American Life Panel (ALP) survey, in which we followed up with approximately 1,900 of our original respondents. In this survey, we asked respondents how often they shopped online in July and August. This survey reflects not only how often people are shopping online and whether they are spending more or less on online shopping, but how shopping behaviors have (or have not) changed since the early days of the COVID-19 pandemic.

We have divided our respondents into three categories on the basis of how often they shop online: frequent (once a week or more), occasional (a few times a month) and infrequent (never or almost never) online shoppers.

In January and February, our respondents were roughly equally split between these categories, as Figure 1 shows. This pattern changed substantially: Online shopping became more common as COVID-19 spread. This change has persisted as the pandemic continues. By August, about 45 percent of our respondents were frequent, one-third were occasional, and only one-quarter were infrequent online shoppers.

By summer 2020, overall trends in online shopping had substantially changed, although these changes were by no means universal. The frequency of online shopping has continued to increase; frequent online shoppers have risen from 35 to 45 percent of all shoppers, even as 55 percent of respondents stuck with their prepandemic habits. Forty percent of our respondents were spending more money online, even as 20 percent were spending less. These trends reinforce what other data show: Although many households have been able to pivot to working and shopping from home, some of those in less-fortunate circumstances are cutting back.

In the August ALP survey, also asked respondents to estimate whether the amount of money that they had spent on online purchases had gone up or down since February. Specifically, we asked respondents whether their spending had doubled, increased by a smaller amount, stayed about the same, or decreased. We cannot calculate exactly how much more or less households are spending, but these responses do provide some sense of changes at the household level.

Thirty-nine percent of Americans reported that they had increased their online spending—11 percent estimated that they had doubled their spending and 28 percent estimated that they had increased it by a smaller amount. Forty-three percent reported spending about the same amount of money, and 19 percent reported spending less.

Unsurprisingly, people who said that they shopped online more frequently were generally spending more on online purchases, although the pattern is not clear-cut. Of those who were shopping online more in July and August, about half were also spending more money. About 42 percent said that their spending had not changed, and 9 percent said that it actually had decreased. Among people who were doing the same amount of online shopping or were shopping online less often, 32 to 35 percent were spending more and about 25 percent were spending less. (ALP surveys, Mayn and Aug. 2020).

SOURCE: Authors‘ calculations using 1,883 responses in the ALP surveys that were conducted in May and August 2020.

NOTE: Respondents were asked the following question: "Over the past month, how often did you do online shopping or get home delivery of any products, including meals, groceries, medication, clothing, books, or other products?" Responses are weighted using sampling weights, as described in Carman and Nataraj, 2020.

Thus, it implies that COVD 19 disease had influenced many US consumers choose to buy any products from online. US Household income seems to be related to spending on online shopping, although perhaps not in the expected direction. Households earning less than $40,000 were more likely to decrease their online spending than higher-income households since March, but they were also most likely to double their online spending within the same time period. It is possible that these households are still spending less in total dollar value than other households, even if they have doubled their spending.

Bibliography

Carman, Katherine Grace, and Shanthi Nataraj, 2020 American Life Panel Survey on Impacts of COVID-19: Technical Documentation, Santa Monica, Calif.: RAND Corporation, RR-A308-1, 2020. As of November 2, 2020: https://www.rand.org/pubs/research_reports/RRA308-1.html

———, 2020 American Life Panel Survey on Impacts of COVID-19: May 2020 Survey Results, Santa Monica, Calif.: RAND Corporation, RR-A308-2-v2, 2020. As of November 2, 2020: https://www.rand.org/pubs/research_reports/RRA308-1.html

———, 2020 American Life Panel Survey on Impacts of COVID-19: August 2020 Survey Results, Santa Monica, Calif.: RAND Corporation, RR-A308-8, 2020. As of November 2, 2020: https://www.rand.org/pubs/research_reports/RRA308-1.html

Cohen, Patricia, Ben Casselman, and Gillian Friedman, "An Extra $600 a Week Kept Many Jobless Workers Afloat. Now What Will They Do?" New York Times, July 29, 2020, updated September 10, 2020.

Thus, COVID 19 disease had influene the global buying habits of shoppers tend to change slowly. Covid-19, however, has been disruptive enough to shake them up, and companies are trying to take advantage.

global businesses need to bring all creatures of habit, and shopping is largely habit-driven. There are very few times in one's life when you have an opportunity to reshape their habits. The classic three are when you get married, when you move home and when you have a baby. And otherwise, your habits are pretty cemented, and you're not really open to forming new habits. And so what this current moment has created is a moment when everyone's habits are up for grabs.

What Is the Risk of Getting COVID-19 While Shopping in order to bring online shopping chance raises?

Whether the shopping is indoors or outdoors, with outdoors being safer the number of people shopping — fewer means it's easier to maintain social (physical) distancing how long you'll take — the faster you're done, the better COVID-19 positivity rate in the local community. So, global many consumers had felt online shopping is more safe to compare to visit shops by COVID 19 disease influence.

The impact of online grocery shopping on food consumer behavior in Covid-19. Some researchers Uses bivariate probit models to empirically investigate the impact of online purchasing channels on Chinese urban consumer food hoarding behaviors with random survey samples. Some research results show that fresh food e-commerce channels are more likely to be associated with panic stockpile behaviors due to higher likelihood of supply shortages than offline channels with government assistance in logistic management. In contrast, community group buy, another format of e-commerce, appears superior in satisfying the consumer needs and easing the panic buying perception.

It suggests that online channels may have diverse impacts on consumers' panic stockpiling behaviors during the extreme situations. Online channels need to develop efficient supply chains to be more resilient to extreme situations and the government shall recognize the increasing share of the online channels together with traditional offline channels when implementing supporting policies. With ever increasing share of online channels, it is imperative in terms of policy implications to understand how would online channels affect hoarding behavior.

Originality/value

They are the first study in online shopping's impact on food stockpile during pandemics using a random sample. Although food stockpile behavior at times of emergency have been investigated in many literature, there are no empirical studies on the impact of online channels on stockpile behaviors under extreme situations. Unlike disasters that immediately impact every entity in supply chains covering producers, vendors, distribution centers and retailers, pandemics did not render supply chains affected immediately, but rather increase consumers‘ willingness to shop online to avoid virus. Thus, Covid-19 provides a natural experiment to investigate the online channels’ impact on stockpile behavior. So, COVID 19 disease may influence many consumers choose to buy foods from online channel.

The situation is rapidly changing. The amount of people deemed safe to gather in a single place has dwindled from thousands, to hundreds, to ten. Restaurants, bars, movie theaters, and gyms in many major cities are shutting down. Meanwhile many office workers are facing new challenges of working remotely full time.

Essentially, people are coming to terms with the realities of our interconnected world and how difficult it is to temporarily separate those connections to others. To say that we are living in unprecedented times feels like an understatement.

One of the responses we’ve seen to how people are approaching this period of isolation and uncertainty is in huge overnight changes to their shopping behaviors. From bulk-buying to online shopping, people are changing what they’re buying, when, and how.

As more cities are going under lockdowns, nonessential businesses are being ordered to close, and customers are generally avoiding public places. Limiting shopping for all but necessary essentials is becoming a new normal. Brands are having to adapt and be flexible to meet changing needs.

This resource is intended to provide information so that you can make the best decisions for your brand during uncertain times. We’ve gathered some facts and numbers around how behaviors are changing, what products people are buying, and what industries are feeling the strain to help you determine what choices you can make for your business.

Understanding Panic Buying and Coronavirus

As news of COVID-19 spread and as it was officially declared a pandemic by the World Health Organization, people responded by stocking up. They bought out medical supplies like hand sanitizer and masks and household essentials like toilet paper and bread. Soon, both brick-and-mortar and online stores were struggling to keep up with demand, and price gouging for supplies became rampant.

Humans respond to crises in different ways. When faced with an uncertain, risky situation over which we have no control, we tend to try whatever we can to feel like we have some control.

Paul Marsden, a consumer psychologist at the University of the Arts London was quoted by CNBC as saying: "Panic buying can be understood as playing to our three fundamental psychology needs." These needs are autonomy (or the need to feel in control of your actions), relatedness (the need to feel that we are doing something to benefit our families), and competence (the need to feel like smart shoppers making the correct choice).

These psychological factors are the same reasons "retail therapy" is a response to many different types of personal crises; however, during a pandemic there are added layers.

One is that the global spread of COVID-19 has been accompanied by a lot of uncertainty and at times contradictory information. When people are hearing differing advice from multiple sources, they have a greater instinct to over-, rather than under-, prepare.

Secondly, there is the crowd mentality. Seeing other people buying up the shelves and then seeing a scarcity of necessary products validates the decision to stock up. No one wants to be left behind without any resources.

Understanding the COVID-19 Effect on Online Shopping Behavio

I don't think it's too soon to say that the COVID-19 global pandemic will likely be one of the defining events of 2020, and that it will have implications that last well into the decade.

The situation is rapidly changing. The amount of people deemed safe to gather in a single place has dwindled from thousands, to hundreds, to ten. Restaurants, bars, movie theaters, and gyms in many major cities are shutting down. Meanwhile many office workers are facing new challenges of working remotely full time.

Essentially, people are coming to terms with the realities of our interconnected world and how difficult it is to temporarily separate those connections to others. To say that we are living in unprecedented times feels like an understatement.

One of the responses we've seen to how people are approaching this period of isolation and uncertainty is in huge overnight changes to their shopping behaviors. From bulk-buying to online shopping, people are changing what they're buying, when, and how.

As more cities are going under lockdowns, nonessential businesses are being ordered to close, and customers are generally avoiding public places.

Limiting shopping for all but necessary essentials is becoming a new normal. Brands are having to adapt and be flexible to meet changing needs.

This resource is intended to provide information so that you can make the best decisions for your brand during uncertain times. We've gathered some facts and numbers around how behaviors are changing, what products people are buying, and what industries are feeling the strain to help you determine what choices you can make for your business.

Understanding Panic Buying and Coronavirus

As news of COVID-19 spread and as it was officially declared a pandemic by the World Health Organization, people responded by stocking up. They bought out medical supplies like hand sanitizer and masks and household essentials like toilet paper and bread. Soon, both brick-and-mortar and online stores were struggling to keep up with demand, and price gouging for supplies became rampant.

Humans respond to crises in different ways. When faced with an uncertain, risky situation over which we have no control, we tend to try whatever we can to feel like we have some control.

Paul Marsden, a consumer psychologist at the University of the Arts London was quoted by CNBC as saying: "Panic buying can be understood as playing to our three fundamental psychology needs." These needs are autonomy (or the need to feel in control of your actions), relatedness (the need to feel that we are doing something to benefit our families), and competence (the need to feel like smart shoppers making the correct choice).

These psychological factors are the same reasons "retail therapy" is a response to many different types of personal crises; however, during a pandemic there are added layers.

One is that the global spread of COVID-19 has been accompanied by a lot of uncertainty and at times contradictory information. When people are hearing differing advice from multiple sources, they have a greater instinct to over-, rather than under-, prepare.

Secondly, there is the crowd mentality. Seeing other people buying up the shelves and then seeing a scarcity of necessary products validates the decision to stock up. No one wants to be left behind without any resources.

While people in general are concerned about the growing pandemic, the youngest generations are particularly altering their purchasing behaviors.

One survey of U.S. and U.K. consumers found that 96% of Millenials and Gen Zs are concerned about the pandemic and its effects on the economy.

This concern is leading them to change their behavior more dramatically than other generations, which includes cutting back on spending, stocking up on items, and spending less on experiences.

2. Gen X and Boomers.

Although still concerned about coronavirus and its effects on the economy, older generations are slightly less concerned than younger generations and letting it impact their shopping habits less. For example, 24% of Boomers and 34% of Gen X said they were letting current events impact what items they purchase, compared to nearly half of Millennials.

COVID-19: Men's and Women's Shopping Behaviors Vary

While data shows that shopping behaviors are changing based on generational differences, we're also seeing variations based on gender.

While survey data shows that women are more likely to be concerned about the effects of COVID-19, it also shows that men are more likely to have it impact their shopping behaviors. One-third of men, compared to 25% of women, reported the pandemic affecting how much they spend on products. Additionally, 36% of men, compared to 28% of women, reported it affecting how much they are spending on experiences (travel, restaurants, entertainment, etc.).

Men were also found to be shopping online and avoiding in-store experiences more than women. This includes taking advantage of options that limit in-store interactions like BOPIS (buy online, pick-up in store), curbside pickup, and subscription services.

Changes in Revenue Across Ecommerce

As people have embraced social distancing as a way to slow the spread of the pandemic, there has naturally been a drop-off in brick-and-mortar shopping. That would seem to mean there would likely be an increase in online shopping as people turn to ecommerce to purchase the items they might have otherwise purchased in person.

Has that prediction won out? In reality, ecommerce sales are not higher across the board, although some industries are seeing significant upticks. This is especially true for online sellers of household goods and groceries. JD.com, China's largest online retailer, has seen sales of common household staples quadruple over the same period last year. A survey by Engine found that people are spending on average 10-30% more online.

1. Grocery ecommerce.

Grocery ecommerce soared in the second week of March, after shoppers turned online to find the goods they needed but weren't available at their local grocery stores. The following graph, with data from Rakuten Intelligence, shows a huge spike in grocery-related ecommerce. The rest of ecommerce seems like it might be up a little bit, but no drastic peaks or valleys.

2. Other ecommerce categories.

In addition to grocery, ecommerce covers a wide number of products, across categories. Common Thread Collective has been providing valuable updates with COVID data on ecommerce shopping behavior, including the chart below. While ecommerce performance is not generally up or down, breaking down the data by vertical tells a bit more of the story.

Understanding the COVID-19 Effect on Online Shopping Behavio

I don't think it's too soon to say that the COVID-19 global pandemic will likely be one of the defining events of 2020, and that it will have implications that last well into the decade.

The situation is rapidly changing. The amount of people deemed safe to gather in a single place has dwindled from thousands, to hundreds, to ten. Restaurants, bars, movie theaters, and gyms in many major cities are shutting down. Meanwhile many office workers are facing new challenges of working remotely full time.

Essentially, people are coming to terms with the realities of our interconnected world and how difficult it is to temporarily separate those connections to others. To say that we are living in unprecedented times feels like an understatement.

One of the responses we've seen to how people are approaching this period of isolation and uncertainty is in huge overnight changes to their shopping behaviors. From bulk-buying to online shopping, people are changing what they're buying, when, and how.

As more cities are going under lockdowns, nonessential businesses are being ordered to close, and customers are generally avoiding public places. Limiting shopping for all but necessary essentials is becoming a new normal. Brands are having to adapt and be flexible to meet changing needs.

This resource is intended to provide information so that you can make the best decisions for your brand during uncertain times. We've gathered some facts and numbers around how behaviors are changing, what products people are buying, and what industries are feeling the strain to help you determine what choices you can make for your business.

Understanding Panic Buying and Coronavirus

As news of COVID-19 spread and as it was officially declared a pandemic by the World Health Organization, people responded by stocking up. They bought out medical supplies like hand sanitizer and masks and household essentials like toilet paper and bread. Soon, both brick-and-mortar and online stores were struggling to keep up with demand, and price gouging for supplies became rampant.

Humans respond to crises in different ways. When faced with an uncertain, risky situation over which we have no control, we tend to try whatever we can to feel like we have some control.

Paul Marsden, a consumer psychologist at the University of the Arts London was quoted by CNBC as saying: "Panic buying can be understood as playing to our three fundamental psychology needs." These needs are autonomy (or the need to feel in control of your actions), relatedness (the need to feel that we are doing something to benefit our families), and competence (the need to feel like smart shoppers making the correct choice).

These psychological factors are the same reasons "retail therapy" is a response to many different types of personal crises; however, during a pandemic there are added layers.

One is that the global spread of COVID-19 has been accompanied by a lot of uncertainty and at times contradictory information. When people are hearing differing advice from multiple sources, they have a greater instinct to over-, rather than under-, prepare.

Secondly, there is the crowd mentality. Seeing other people buying up the shelves and then seeing a scarcity of necessary products validates the decision to stock up. No one wants to be left behind without any resources.

Has that prediction won out? In reality, ecommerce sales are not higher across the board, although some industries are seeing significant upticks. This is especially true for online sellers of household goods and groceries. JD.com, China's largest online retailer, has seen sales of common household staples quadruple over the same period last year. A survey by Engine found that people are spending on average 10-30% more online.

1. Grocery ecommerce.

Grocery ecommerce soared in the second week of March, after shoppers turned online to find the goods they needed but weren't available at their local grocery stores. The following graph, with data from Rakuten Intelligence, shows a huge spike in grocery-related ecommerce. The rest of ecommerce seems like it might be up a little bit, but no drastic peaks or valleys.

2. Other ecommerce categories.

In addition to grocery, ecommerce covers a wide number of products, across categories. Common Thread Collective has been providing valuable updates with COVID data on ecommerce shopping behavior, including the chart below. While ecommerce performance is not generally up or down, breaking down the data by vertical tells a bit more of the story.

3. Subscription services.

While ecommerce sales do not generally appear to be skyrocketing as one might expect, there are some exceptions. One of these is in subscription and convenience services, which have seen significant upward trends in both revenue and conversion.

Anyone who has faced empty shelves or seen price gouging online knows that health and safety products are being purchased far faster than they can be produced and restocked.

According to data from Nielsen, items like hygienic and medical mask sales are up by more than 300%.

2. Shelf-stable goods.

Another category of consumer packaged goods that is booming is shelf-stable items. These fit into the category of people planning for long-term quarantine. According to Nielsen, products like shelf-stable milk and milk substitutes (particularly oat milk) are up by more than 300% in dollar growth. Other items seeing increases are things like dried beans and fruit snacks that have a long shelf life.

3. Food and beverage.

In addition to long-term quarantine type items, for groceries in general, sales are up. However, there are some behavioral changes around the way people are buying groceries.

For example, in an effort to avoid crowds at supermarkets, many people are choosing BOPIS (buy-online-pick-up-in-store) or delivery options. Downloads of apps like Instacart and Shipt that allow people to hire personal shoppers to prepare and in some cases deliver their grocery orders have increased by between 124% (for Shipt) and 218% (for Instacart). People are also choosing to buy these items from online stores more than they did prior.

Shipbob, a shipping and fulfillment partner for ecommerce stores, gathered data from 3,000+ of their merchants and is tracking the data.

While the chart below shows some fluctuations, the month-over-month increase in online sales for food and beverage is 18.8%

4. Digital streaming.

While less about the immediacy of protecting and feeding themselves, it comes as no surprise that as people are homebound and no longer pursuing external entertainment options that there is an increase in digital streaming services. In addition to streaming services like Netflix, Amazon, Hulu, and Disney+ seeing atypical gains in subscribers in the first quarter of 2020, non-traditional streaming services like movie studios are releasing media streaming, on-demand, sometimes earlier than projected release.

5. Luxury goods.

While the above products and services are increasing in sales due to the current situation, other industries are not doing as well. In addition to obvious ones like entertainment, restaurants, and travel, one area projected to have significant losses is the luxury goods industry.

Vogue Business projects a potential loss as great as $10 billion for this industry in 2020 due to COVID-19. This is in part because luxury goods rely heavily on the Asian market's purchasing power, where the pandemic has been affecting consumers since January.

Understanding the COVID-19 Effect on Online Shopping Behavior

The situation is rapidly changing. The amount of people deemed safe to gather in a single place has dwindled from thousands, to hundreds, to ten. Restaurants, bars, movie theaters, and gyms in many major cities are shutting down. Meanwhile many office workers are facing new challenges of working remotely full time.

Essentially, people are coming to terms with the realities of our interconnected world and how difficult it is to temporarily separate those connections to others. To say that we are living in unprecedented times feels like an understatement.

One of the responses we've seen to how people are approaching this period of isolation and uncertainty is in huge overnight changes to their shopping behaviors. From bulk-buying to online shopping, people are changing what they're buying, when, and how.

As more cities are going under lockdowns, nonessential businesses are being ordered to close, and customers are generally avoiding public places. Limiting shopping for all but necessary essentials is becoming a new normal. Brands are having to adapt and be flexible to meet changing needs.

This resource is intended to provide information so that you can make the best decisions for your brand during uncertain times. We've gathered some facts and numbers around how behaviors are changing, what products people are buying, and what industries are feeling the strain to help you determine what choices you can make for your business.

Understanding Panic Buying and Coronavirus

As news of COVID-19 spread and as it was officially declared a pandemic by the World Health Organization, people responded by stocking up. They bought out medical supplies like hand sanitizer and masks and household essentials like toilet paper and bread. Soon, both brick-and-mortar and online stores were struggling to keep up with demand, and price gouging for supplies became rampant.

Humans respond to crises in different ways. When faced with an uncertain, risky situation over which we have no control, we tend to try whatever we can to feel like we have some control.

Paul Marsden, a consumer psychologist at the University of the Arts London was quoted by CNBC as saying: "Panic buying can be understood as playing to our three fundamental psychology needs." These needs are autonomy (or the need to feel in control of your actions), relatedness (the need to feel that we are doing something to benefit our families), and competence (the need to feel like smart shoppers making the correct choice).

These psychological factors are the same reasons "retail therapy" is a response to many different types of personal crises; however, during a pandemic there are added layers.

One is that the global spread of COVID-19 has been accompanied by a lot of uncertainty and at times contradictory information. When people are hearing differing advice from multiple sources, they have a greater instinct to over-, rather than under-, prepare.

Secondly, there is the crowd mentality. Seeing other people buying up the shelves and then seeing a scarcity of necessary products validates the decision to stock up. No one wants to be left behind without any resources.

COVID-19 is Changing the Ecommerce Landscape.

Retail businesses around the world over are being affected by COVID-19 through everything from rapidly changing customer behavior to supply issues.

We're offering a snapshot of the data around these changes and how businesses are adapting to them.

COVID-19: Men's and Women's Shopping Behaviors Vary

While data shows that shopping behaviors are changing based on generational differences, we're also seeing variations based on gender.

While survey data shows that women are more likely to be concerned about the effects of COVID-19, it also shows that men are more likely to have it impact their shopping behaviors. One-third of men, compared to 25% of women, reported the pandemic affecting how much they spend on products. Additionally, 36% of men, compared to 28% of women, reported it affecting how much they are spending on experiences (travel, restaurants, entertainment, etc.).

Men were also found to be shopping online and avoiding in-store experiences more than women. This includes taking advantage of options that limit in-store interactions like BOPIS (buy online, pick-up in store), curbside pickup, and subscription services.

Changes in Revenue Across Ecommerce

As people have embraced social distancing as a way to slow the spread of the pandemic, there has naturally been a drop-off in brick-and-mortar shopping. That would seem to mean there would likely be an increase in online shopping as people turn to ecommerce to purchase the items they might have otherwise purchased in person.

Has that prediction won out? In reality, ecommerce sales are not higher across the board, although some industries are seeing significant upticks. This is especially true for online sellers of household goods and groceries. JD.com, China's largest online retailer, has seen sales of common household staples quadruple over the same period last year. A survey by Engine found that people are spending on average 10-30% more online.

1. Grocery ecommerce.

Grocery ecommerce soared in the second week of March, after shoppers turned online to find the goods they needed but weren't available at their local grocery stores. The following graph, with data from Rakuten Intelligence, shows a huge spike in grocery-related ecommerce. The rest of ecommerce seems like it might be up a little bit, but no drastic peaks or valleys.

Source

2. Other ecommerce categories.

In addition to grocery, ecommerce covers a wide number of products, across categories. Common Thread Collective has been providing valuable updates with COVID data on ecommerce shopping behavior, including the chart below. While ecommerce performance is not generally up or down, breaking down the data by vertical tells a bit more of the story.

Source: Common Thread Collective

1. Health and safety products.

Anyone who has faced empty shelves or seen price gouging online knows that health and safety products are being purchased far faster than they can be produced and restocked.

According to data from Nielsen, items like hygienic and medical mask sales are up by more than 300%.

Health and safety products chart

2. Shelf-stable goods.

Another category of consumer packaged goods that is booming is shelf-stable items. These fit into the category of people planning for long-term quarantine. According to Nielsen, products like shelf-stable milk and milk substitutes (particularly oat milk) are up by more than 300% in dollar growth. Other items seeing increases are things like dried beans and fruit snacks that have a long shelf life.

3. Food and beverage.

In addition to long-term quarantine type items, for groceries in general, sales are up. However, there are some behavioral changes around the way people are buying groceries.

For example, in an effort to avoid crowds at supermarkets, many people are choosing BOPIS (buy-online-pick-up-in-store) or delivery options. Downloads of apps like Instacart and Shipt that allow people to hire personal shoppers to prepare and in some cases deliver their grocery orders have increased by between 124% (for Shipt) and 218% (for Instacart). People are also choosing to buy these items from online stores more than they did prior.

Shipbob, a shipping and fulfillment partner for ecommerce stores, gathered data from 3,000+ of their merchants and is tracking the data. While the chart below shows some fluctuations, the month-over-month increase in online sales for food and beverage is 18.8%

4. Digital streaming.

While less about the immediacy of protecting and feeding themselves, it comes as no surprise that as people are homebound and no longer pursuing external entertainment options that there is an increase in digital streaming services. In addition to streaming services like Netflix, Amazon, Hulu, and Disney+ seeing atypical gains in subscribers in the first quarter of 2020, non-traditional streaming services like movie studios are releasing media streaming, on-demand, sometimes earlier than projected release.

5. Luxury goods.

While the above products and services are increasing in sales due to the current situation, other industries are not doing as well. In addition to obvious ones like entertainment, restaurants, and travel, one area projected to have significant losses is the luxury goods industry.

Vogue Business projects a potential loss as great as $10 billion for this industry in 2020 due to COVID-19. This is in part because luxury goods rely heavily on the Asian market's purchasing power, where the pandemic has been affecting consumers since January.

6. Fashion and apparel.

As mentioned above, omnichannel sellers are seeing big losses, in part because they're closing the retail arms of their businesses all together. People are understandably not interested in shopping for clothes in person. Department stores like Macy's and JCPenney, large chains like Abercrombie & Fitch and Nike, and DTC brands with some storefronts like Rothys and Everlane are all closing their physical stores and experiencing losses. Some stores like Patagonia are halting even their online stores to protect all workers in their supply chain.

Even online apparel sales are down as people are putting more of their budgets into daily essentials. The chart below is again from Shipbob's data of their 3,000+ merchants. This shows an overall 20% decrease in sales month-over-month.

COVID 19 disease how impacts global economic recession
on shopping aspect

The COVID-19 pandemic has had far-reaching economic consequences beyond the spread of the disease itself and efforts to quarantine it. As the SARS-CoV-2 virus has spread around the globe, concerns have shifted from supply-side manufacturing issues to decreased business in the services sector. The pandemic caused the largest global recession in history, with more than a third of the global population at the time being placed on lockdown. Supply shortages are expected to affect a number of sectors due to panic buying, increased usage of goods to fight the pandemic, and disruption to factories and logistics in mainland China. There have been instances of price gouging.There have been widespread reports of shortages of pharmaceuticals, with many areas seeing panic buying and consequent shortages of food and other essential grocery items.The technology industry, in particular, has been warning about delays to shipments of electronic goods.

By COVID 19 disease influences to global economy losses, Economic recovery programmes are began to implement by EU countries

Some economic recovery programmes include Next Generation EU and Pandemic Emergency Purchase Programme. A study published in August 2020 concluded that the direct effect of the response to the pandemic on global warming will likely be negligible and that a well-designed economic recovery could avoid future warming of 0.3 °C by 2050. The study indicates that systemic change for "decarbonization" of humanity's economic structures is required for a substantial impact on global warming, which also has economic aspects. Beyond targeted financing of green projects or sectors, contemporary decision-making mechanisms also allow for excluding projects with substantial environmental, social, or climate risks from financial relief. Over 260 civil society organizations called on Chinese actors to ensure that COVID-19 related Belt and Road Initiative funding excludes such projects.In November 2020 the IMF said that governments and central banks had promised $19.5 trillion of support since the coronavirus began.

Food crisis on agricultural aspect influences by COVID 19 disease

In food crisis countries, up to 80 percent of the population relies on agriculture for their livelihoods. Therefore, any further disruptions to food production and related value chains, for example in the form of reduced availability of critical inputs or restricted access to lands or markets, could be catastrophic for vulnerable populations.The agriculture sector plays an important role in influencing migratory patterns. Transhumant pastoral populations are likely to be hard hit by any border closures, as they rely on seasonal movements of livestock for their food and income. The disruption of traditional and western patterns and the creation of new ones may lead to tensions and even violent conflicts between resident and pastoralist communities, resulting in local displacement and increased levels of poverty and food insecurity.

According to FAO, it is crucial to maintain and support the continuous functioning of local food markets, value chains and agri-food systems in food crisis contexts, including through ongoing and scaled up support to food processing, transport, marketing, and so forth; strengthening of local producers' groups to maintain negotiation power and access to markets; and, advocating for trade corridors to remain open as much as possible during COVID-19 related movement restrictions.

COVID 19 diease how influences global financial market

Economic turmoil associated with the coronavirus pandemic has wide-ranging and severe impacts upon financial markets, including stock, bond and commodity (including crude oil and gold) markets. Major events included the Russia–Saudi Arabia oil price war that resulted in a collapse of crude oil prices and a stock market crash in March 2020. The United Nations Development Programme expects a US$220 billion reduction in revenue in developing countries, and expects COVID-19's economic impact to last for months or even years.[46][30] Some expect natural gas prices to fall.

COVID 19 hoe influences global manufacturing

New vehicle sales in the United States have declined by 40%. The American Big Three have all shut down their US factories. The German automotive industry came into the crisis after having already suffered from the Dieselgate-scandal, as well as competition from electric cars. Boeing and Airbus suspended production at some factories. A survey conducted by the British Plastics Federation (BPF) explored how COVID-19 is impacting manufacturing businesses in the United Kingdom (UK). Over 80% of respondents anticipated a decline in turnover over the next 2 quarters, with 98% admitting concern about the negative impact of the pandemic on business operations.

Impact of the COVID-19 pandemic on the arts and cultural heritage, entertainment and sport lesiure industry

The epidemic had a sudden and substantial impact on the arts and cultural heritage (GLAM) sectors worldwide. The global health crisis and the uncertainty resulting from it profoundly affected organisations' operations as well as individuals – both employed and independent – across the sector. By March 2020, across the world most cultural institutions had been indefinitely closed (or at least with their services radically curtailed) exhibitions, events and performances cancelled or postponed. Many individuals temporarily or permanently lost contracts or employment with varying degrees of warning and financial assistance available. Equally, financial stimulus from governments and charities for artists, have provided greatly differing levels of support, depending on the sector and the country.

In countries such as Australia, where the arts contributed to about 6.4% of GDP, effects on individuals and the economy have been significant.

The impact of COVID 19 disease how influences global cinema entertainment industry

The pandemic has impacted the film industry. Across the world and to varying degrees, cinemas have been closed, festivals have been cancelled or postponed, and film releases have been moved to future dates. As cinemas closed, the global box office dropped by billions of dollars, while streaming became more popular and the stock of Netflix rose; the stock of film exhibitors dropped dramatically. Almost all blockbusters to be released after the March opening weekend were postponed or cancelled around the world, with film productions also halted. Massive losses in the industry have been predicted.

The impact of COVD 19 disease infuences to television and video game entetainment industry, they have similar consumer behavior , this disease excits many young and old age audiences choose to watch movies at homes and young age people choose to buy video game to play at homes.

The COVID-19 pandemic has shut down or delayed production of television programs in several countries.[citation needed] However, a joint report from Apptopia and Braze showed a 30.7% increase in streaming sessions worldwide on platforms such as Disney+, Netflix, and Hulu during the month of March.

The pandemic also affected the video game sector to a smaller degree. As the outbreak appeared in China first, supply chains affected the manufacturing and production of some video game consoles, delaying their releases and making current supplies scarcer. As the outbreak and pandemic spread, several keystone trade events, including E3 2020, were cancelled over concerns of further spread. The economic impact on the video game sector is not expected to be as large as in film or other entertainment sectors as much of the work in video game production can be decentralised and performed remotely, and products distributed digitally to consumers regardless of various national and regional lockdowns on businesses and services.

How CVID 19 disease influences publish industry, it influences many readers choose to read e-books from home computer, they do not like to visit book shops to buy books.

In light of the public health situation in which includes afflicted regions where retail sectors deemed non-essential have been ordered closed for the interim, Diamond Comic Distributors announced on 24 March 2020 a full suspension of distributing published material and related merchandise as 1 April 2020 until further notice. As Diamond has a near-monopoly on printed comic book distribution, this is described as an "extinction-level event" that threatens to drive the entire specialized comic book retail sector out of business with that one move. As a result, publishers like IDW Publishing and Dark Horse Comics have suspended publication of their periodicals while DC Comics is exploring distribution alternatives including an increased focus on online retail of digital material.

COVID 19 disease influences online shopping has more customers global. The pandemic has impacted the retail sector. Shopping centres around the world responded by reducing hours or closing down temporarily. As of 18 March 2020, the footfall to shopping centres fell by up to 30%, with significant impact in every continent.Additionally, product demand exceeded supply for many consumables, resulting in empty retail shelves.In Australia, the pandemic has provided a new opportunity for daigou shoppers to re-sell into the China market.

Some retailers have employed contactless home delivery or curbside pickup for items purchased through e-commerce sites.By April, retailers had started implementing "retail to go" models where consumers could pick up their orders. An estimated 40% of shoppers were shopping online and choosing to pick up in-store, a behavior that had suddenly doubled as compared to the previous year.

Small-scale farmers have been embracing digital technologies as a way to directly sell produce, and community-supported agriculture and direct-sell delivery systems are on the rise. For Amazon ecommerce example, it help Amazon increases many online consumers. Many traditional visiting shops consumers began to choose to apply internet channel to buy any products. In mid-April, Amazon confirmed that workers at over half of its 110 U.S. warehouses had been diagnosed with coronavirus.On 16 June, the United States Department of Commerce announced that retail sales for the month of May had seen an increase of 17.7% from April as states began to reopen and lift restrictions. According to CNBC, This marks the biggest one month jump in the history of retailing in the United States. Numbers for June reflected a 7.5 percent rise in sales. So, it causes many shops close, due to many visting shop customers began to accept to apply internet or online channel to buy any products to replace visiting shops purchase method.

Hence, instead of COVID 19 disease influences tourism recession, it also brings many shops close, but it creates new online purchase model to excite many traditional visiting shop purchase consumers began to choose online purchase model in retail aspect. But it also influences many restaurants close, because many people feel fear to go to restaurants to eat, due to food environment may be one most serious COVID 19 disease places. So, many people choose to buy food to cook at home, so, supermarkets may be one attractive place to let us to choose to buy food more safe to compare restaurants. Thus, COVID 19 disease may cause some kinds of businesses close , but it also bring new chance to some kinds of businesses.

When economy recovers after COVID disease disappears

Firstly, we need to know how Long Does Immunity Last After COVID-19? Then, we can analyze whether when global economy may recover in possible when COVID 19 disease can disappear in future one day. For those who recover from COVID-19, new research shows immunity to the virus can last for at least 8 months, and may last much longer. Understanding how our immune system responds to the virus is an important step in vaccine development. Currently two vaccines, from Pfizer-BioNTech and Moderna, are authorized for use in the United States. Several other promising vaccines are also in development, but until they become widely available we must practice physical distancing and mask-wearing to keep transmission down.

How Fast Can the U.S. Economy Recover From COVID-19?

We expect U.S. GDP to fall 5.1% in 2020. This is far worse than the Great Recession. Before jumping to pessimistic conclusions, however, investors should consider a much more important issue: What is the recovery going to look like? We expect robust catch-up growth in the years following 2020. By 2024, we think that the U.S. GDP level will recover to just 1% below our pre-COVID-19 expectation.
Our analysis of the history of global recessions showed that many recessions don't have a long-run negative impact on the economy. The worst recessions in terms of long-run impact (the Great Depression or the Great Recession) are generally the product of persistent economic policy error.

But economic policy response has been extremely impressive so far in 2020, especially the United States' historically large fiscal stimulus.

Fiscal stimulus is already lifting up U.S. economic activity substantially. Stimulus provided a massive boost to personal disposable incomes in April. Though much of the extra income was saved, more detailed analysis shows that the stimulus payments still boosted spending. Meanwhile, the extra savings means that household and firm balance sheets will be in good shape to spend more as the economy recovers.

We expect broad availability of a vaccine to erase COVID-19's direct impact on the U.S. and global economies by mid-2021. The need to social distance will continue to weigh heavily on some parts of the economy (with the hardest-hit constituting about 5% of GDP) through the rest of 2020. However, positive data about the vaccine's efficacy should arrive in the second half of 2020, bolstering consumer and business confidence and promoting a broader recovery in the economy.

U.S. Can Mount Solid Recovery in Second Half Even as COVID-19 Drags Highly on Some Sectors

We think a crucial perspective in modeling the near-term trajectory of the U.S. economy is to look at the industry level, as different industries are seeing disparate impact from the pandemic. We group U.S. industries into three broad categories based on direct impact from COVID-19: highest affected (such as restaurants and hotels), moderately affected (such as retail or healthcare), and other industries.

While the U.S. doesn't issue timely GDP statistics on each industry, we can use the employment figures to gauge industry trends in economic activity. Based on the data through May, we project that total U.S. employment will be down 12.5% in the second quarter overall. We think the highest-affected industries will see a 37% hit. Within each industry, we think the fall in GDP will surpass the fall in employment, owing to labor hoarding (companies retaining more workers than needed to carry out operations). In particular, the Paycheck Protection Program strongly encourages companies to hold on to excess workers. Despite this, we expect the aggregate fall in GDP to be less than the fall in employment, as the industries being hit hardest have a much higher share of employment than GDP. The highest-affected industries (for example restaurants, which have a low level of output per worker) account for 15% of U.S. payroll employment though just 6% of U.S. GDP. Altogether, we expect a 10.6% drop in second-quarter GDP (36% on an "annualized" basis, which is most widely quoted in the media).

We expect a sharp GDP rebound in the second half of 2020, with 5.9% growth in the third quarter and 3.2% growth in the fourth quarter (nonannualized). We don't think the need for social distancing will disappear in the second half of 2020, as COVID-19 will still be a lingering threat until a vaccine is broadly available, which we project will occur in the first half of 2021. Still, even while social distancing weighs on highly affected industries, we think the rest of the economy can cope with the ongoing pandemic.

The problem with both the U.S. economy in general and the labor market in particular is not a lack of government stimulus — it's the coronavirus. People are either afraid to work or state governments, to fight the virus, are locking down the businesses where they would work.

As a result, more than 10.7 million people remain out of work and the unemployment rate sits at a relatively high 6.7 percent (although down from 14.7 percent in April). The lockdowns have been particularly hard on the small businesses that employ many of these people. For example, 110,000 restaurants have closed permanently and 500,000 others are in serious trouble, according to a recent National Restaurant Association survey.

Economic recovery after COVID-19: the impact on labor and financial markets

The patterns of COVID-19 infection are differing widely across countries and markets. This in turn affects economic outcomes. In this blog we reflect on these differing outcomes and what they might mean for the pace of global economic recovery. Governments around the world have taken different policy stances and strategies for handling the coronavirus pandemic, depending on their circumstances. In this blog, I do not comment on the political response - but make clear that the containment of the virus should be the upmost priority.

There has been considerable debate as to what the shape of economic recovery might look like. Optimistic scenarios point to a rapid "V" shaped recovery, while more pessimistic viewpoints suggest a "U" or even an "L" shaped recovery. While such scenarios are useful in characterizing some of the key issues facing all economies affected by COVID-19, they are also simplistic – recovery patterns are trending differently across key markets (financial, non-financial and labor).

Variable trends across different markets will not combine in an even manner due to inherent differences in each market, their relative health pre-COVID-19 and the design and prioritization of government policy initiatives designed to help offset the health and economic crises.

The most realistic recovery scenario is shaped like a "kinked V" – an initial sharp decline in market activity, followed by a relatively swift bounce back towards pre-COVID-19 levels (once lockdown measures are eased). However, this bounce back won't occur in full. Given the scale of the initial decline most markets will experience long term scarring, meaning that after the initial bounce back there will be an elongated period before markets return fully to pre-COVID-19 levels.

After examining a wide range of data across multiple market segments, differences between the presence and timing of the kinked-V can be seen most starkly in financial and labor markets. These are discussed in turn, but the essence is that in some financial markets the kinked-V has already manifested itself, meaning that they have largely returned to where they were before the pandemic. Labor markets, however, lag significantly behind with evidence from previous recessions illustrating that it may take as long as a decade for normality to return – if at all.

In the more optimistic outcome - the "V-shape": workers' expectations regarding a rapid return to work are fulfilled and only a small proportion become long term unemployed. In the pessimistic outcome - the "L-shape": a high proportion of workers who are temporarily furloughed are not recalled to their pre-COVID-19 job roles. This means they must re-enter the labour market, spend time on job search and possibly even re-skill. This outcome would lead to a much longer recovery timeline.

Perhaps the most likely outcome is somewhere between the two. Initial, tentative signs of a bounce back can be seen in the US unemployment data. In Chart 2, 2020 data for May and June show a rapid reduction in unemployment levels of 13.3% and 11.1% respectively – a +3% shift even with lockdowns still in place in many US states. This is well ahead of the Hall and Kudlyak estimates.

However, a combination of a broad range of factors might limit this bounce back and point to a kinked-V recovery more in line with Hall and Kudlyak. Factors driving the slower paced recovery could be: employer cost-cutting measures leading to job destruction, fundamental changes in working process needed to prevent the spread of COVID-19, the structurally weak state of labor markets and household earnings growth going into the COVID-19 crises, the time-lags and costs associated with re-skilling and a sharp adjustment in how workers and employers use their workforces (e.g. more working from home, streamlined operational processes etc.).

The contrasts between the pace of adjustments in financial and labor markets are stark, but perhaps also unsurprising. While stock market indices seem to be recovering quite quickly, the labor market effects could take a up to a decade to be fully realized. The question then becomes: what scale of feedback loop is there between these two markets? A weaker labor market will put further downward pressure on product and service demand which could in turn lead to hysteresis, weaker equity markets, lower business earnings and reduced overall economic growth.

While the risk of a full downward employment-demand-price spiral (a hysteresis type effect) is relatively low, it could manifest itself in lower incomes for poorer households and widening inequality which was one of the key outcomes of the 2008 crisis. A second-round feedback loop into financial markets should also not be ruled out as this picture becomes clearer. Policy makers should seek to avoid this outcome and invest now in bolstering labor market opportunities for those whose jobs and earnings potential are negatively affected by the COVID-19 crisis.

While the labor market is certainly not as vibrant as it was in 2019, both the number of people unemployed and the unemployment rate are at about the same level they were in early 2014, a full five years into President Barack Obama's administration and 4½ years after the recession ended. I doubt that then-Vice President Biden thought that was a jobs crisis.

Even during the pandemic, the economy has generated a historic increase of 12.3 million jobs since April. The third quarter's 33.1 percent gross domestic product growth rate was an unexpected historic high, and the Atlanta Fed's GDPNow model is forecasting a very strong growth rate, 11.2 percent, for the fourth quarter.

There are already jobs available that could be filled if people felt safe working. At the end of October (the most recent month for which data is available), the economy had 6.7 million job openings. That's more than in any month during the entire Obama administration, and over a million more than when Obama and Biden left office. The real crisis is a lack of workers, not a lack of jobs.

According to the National Federation of Independent Businesses' monthly survey for the end of November, finding qualified employees was the No. 1 problem businesses faced. Nearly half of these businesses hired or tried to hire employees, and nearly 90 percent of them reported few or no qualified applicants.

For now, though, with the approval and widespread distribution of coronavirus vaccines, the U.S. economy would be free to soar as Americans return to work, with no need for even more government stimulus spending. But that will happen only if the next president resists the urge to use the pandemic to "fundamentally transform" America by implementing programs that swell the government rather than the economy.

India's economy shows signs of recovery as Covid-19 cases decline

Business Activity Activity in India's dominant services sector expanded for a third straight month in December, although at a slower pace. The Markit India Services Purchasing Managers' Index came in at 52.3 in December from 53.7 a month earlier.

Consumer Activity Passenger vehicle sales, a key indicator of demand, rose nearly 14% in December from a year ago, with two-wheeler sales witnessing robust growth. The Reserve Bank of India said in its latest monthly bulletin that the employment s...

Industrial Activity Industrial production shrank 1.9% in November from a year earlier. Production of capital goods declined 7.1%, although infrastructure and construction goods showed a slight expansion of 0.7% from a year ago.

On conclusion, it seems that India's economy ought may have rapid recover more than US's economy after COVID 19 disease disappears because, during nowadays COVID 19 disease is happening, India's economy is significant more stable to compare US's economy nowadays. So, I believe that when COVID 19 disease disappears, India's economy can recover more rapid and easier to compare US's economy. So, illness may bring online shopping demand increase, due to many consumers like to stay at home to avoid illness as well as travel demand reduces because many travelers feel fear to go to other countries to travel , due to illness influences.

www.ingramcontent.com/pod-product-compliance
Ingram Content Group UK Ltd.
Pitfield, Milton Keynes, MK11 3LW, UK
UKHW021921190726
13853UKWH00002B/770

9 798888 498514